ASK
SUZE

. . . ABOUT DEBT

ALSO BY SUZE ORMAN

You've Earned It, Don't Lose It
The 9 Steps to Financial Freedom
The Courage to Be Rich

Riverhead Books
a member of
Penguin Putnam Inc.
New York
2000

ASK SUZE

—◆—

...ABOUT DEBT

SUZE ORMAN

This publication is designed to provide accurate and authoritative information in regard to the subject matter covered. It is published with the understanding that the publisher and author are not engaged in rendering legal, accounting, or other professional service. If legal advice or other professional advice, including financial, is required, the services of a competent professional person should be sought.

RIVERHEAD BOOKS
a member of
Penguin Putnam Inc.
375 Hudson Street
New York, NY 10014

ISBN 1-57322-421-9
GEN-837

Printed in the United States of America
1   3   5   7   9   10   8   6   4   2

This book is printed on acid-free paper. ∞

Book design by Deborah Kerner and Claire Vaccaro

ACKNOWLEDGMENTS

I'd like to thank Peter J. Smith for his
help in compiling this book.

INTRODUCTION

If you are not in debt of some kind, you're a pretty unusual person. For many of us, debt is a part—sometimes an overwhelming part—of our financial lives. How could it not be? Nowadays we don't have to go to the credit card companies, they come directly to us—sometimes even calling us at home. Two, three, four different offers show up in our mail every month, telling us that we're "pre-approved," leading us to think that all we have to do is fill out the application and then we can buy that CD player or that new computer we've been eyeing. It's hard to resist these tempting offers, and most people fall victim to them.

To put it frankly, credit card companies are in the business of separating you from your money. They know exactly how to lure you deeper and deeper into trouble. In fact, they practically have it down to a science. If you're one of the many among us susceptible to credit card debt, have you ever noticed that when your "available credit" is going down, all of a sudden you get a letter in the mail, telling you that because you're such an unbelievably good customer, the credit card company is raising your credit limit by $2,000? What a thoughtful company, you tell yourself! You feel flattered that you're considered such a good credit risk.

But let's think about the logic the credit card company is really applying to your situation: Here's a customer who's already racked up $5,000 worth of credit card debt, and who now is getting low on available credit. This customer's credit report shows that he'll go nearly all the way to his credit limit—so, hey, why not give him an extra $2,000 to spend? That way we can earn interest on $7,000 rather than $5,000. And when this person maxes out his card next time, we'll raise his credit limit again! But we'll frame our letter to him in such a way that he feels good about himself. . . .

In my opinion, debt is bondage. It weighs down your spirits, occupies your mind day and night, and makes you feel backed into a corner. This is something I can personally attest to, because I've been in debt myself. In my own case, debt drove me into a state of denial. To keep up appearances when money got tight, I charged more and more. And then my debt became a secret—a private, shameful thing I hid from others. But in public I was still picking up the tabs for my friends, buying expensive gifts, trying to be more by spending more. I've spoken publicly about my debt quite often in recent years, in an effort to get people to "come clean" to their friends and families about their spending dependencies and break the dangerous cycle of denial. Debt, far more than we realize, is all around us.

There are two kinds of debt, personal and institutional. Personal debt is money you owe to a family member, a friend, or any other human being. Institutional debt is money you owe to a credit card company, a business, a college, the IRS, a bank or credit union, and so on. Whichever kind of debt you have right now, whether personal or institutional or a combination of the two, it undermines everything in your life—particularly your ability to save and to invest in your future. And in the worst of all possible cases, it can bankrupt you.

The following questions and answers are offered as a way for you to start to help yourself out of debt. It is of the utmost importance that you be honest with yourself and your loved ones about your situation. Relieving yourself of the burden of secrecy will lighten your load immediately. With the support of those close to you and the right information, you will soon begin to reclaim your life, one of the richest, most empowering states of being there is.

THE EMOTIONS OF DEBT

How do I know if I'm in trouble with debt?
If you can't pay off all your debt right this minute, whether it's a personal loan you arranged with your brother or a $3,000 balance you owe to various credit card companies, you're in trouble. I know this sounds harsh, but on some level it is true. Everyone who has massive debt today started out with a small balance and thought they could handle the monthly payments, but before they knew it, they owed more and more and more. I have learned that if you cannot pay your credit card bills in full at the end of every month, you are asking for trouble.

Why is it that so many people get into financial trouble?
People get into debt for a lot of different reasons, but I have often noticed a correlation—an inverse relationship—between self-esteem and debt. I call it your debt set point. The lower your self-esteem, the higher your debt set point. If you feel

generally great about yourself and are dealing with your life in an honest, responsible way, chances are you don't have a lot of outstanding debt. But if you are spending more money than you have, you are probably spending money not only to have more but to *be* more. The less self-esteem you have, the more debt you create.

What do you mean by my "debt set point"?

Your set point is your personal bottom. Think of it as your own personal credit limit. It's the point at which you are finally willing to put a stop to all this credit card madness. Each of us has our own set point. It could be $2,000 or it could be $25,000, but the odds are good that you'll know yours when you reach it. There comes a time when we decide to stop the downward plunge—it may be before or after we hit bottom. That is your set point. It can be terrifying when you reach it, but in the end it is a blessed relief, since it forces us to take decisive, positive action.

But remember, working on your debt includes working on why you got into debt in the first place. This usually involves working on your self-esteem, defining who you are rather than what you have. Remind yourself that you are not a bad person simply because you have credit card debt. You are simply a person who has managed your money badly. Big difference! And again, I ask you to tell someone—someone you trust—about your credit card debt. It is an important way to begin dealing truly and honestly with your credit card debt.

Are there other personality traits that put a person at risk, debtwise?

That's not so simple to answer, but in my experience I've found that people with large amounts of debt often avoid looking themselves—and their debt—squarely in the eye. Sometimes they are people who have problems with impulse control. When they see an item in a store, they just have to have it, no matter whether they need it or can afford it. People who grew up without much money in their household and who later make a good living sometimes spend too much to make up for everything they didn't get when they were children—without even realizing it. People who feel entitled to the good life, or who are unconsciously copying a mother or father who lived beyond her or his means can be prone to credit card trouble, too. If you feel you need to impress people with what you have rather than who you are, then you are at high risk for credit card abuse. It's also worth noting that debt doesn't discriminate; it afflicts the rich and poor alike.

Is there ever a time in life when it's okay to have debt?
Yes. Debt has a time and a place in all our lives, but your debt must be in alignment with the goals you've set for yourself. For example, do you want to pursue your dream of attending college? Then a student loan that will help finance your college education is "good debt" since it is in alignment with your future aspirations. What about the mortgage you're carrying on the house you've fallen in love with, the one that is not beyond your means? That's good debt, too, since it enables you to pursue the dream of home ownership and to create a safe haven for yourself and your family. What about the loan you took out two years ago to help your parents get through a rough financial patch or a health scare? Or the car loan you've applied for, assuming you need a car and can afford the payments? Or the money you borrowed from your sister to cover a specific cash-flow crunch when you know for certain that the money will be coming in and you'll be able to pay her back by a specific date? In my opinion, all these loan situations are good, proud, worthy, and honorable.

On the other hand, overspending on your credit cards merely to accumulate new clothes to show off, to keep pace with your friends' spending and acquisitions, is lousy debt, negative debt. It's sacrificing tomorrow's needs to today's desires.

CREDIT CARD BASICS

Credit cards are a staple of modern life, and rightfully so. They allow consumers a flexible, convenient way to purchase things we need and want. Credit cards also allow us to make purchases with money we don't yet have, and that's where things can get tricky. If we are careful about which cards we get, what their rates and terms are, and how we use them, credit cards and their relatives (such as charge cards and debit cards) can be very useful. But they are also dangerous—not only because they tempt us into buying more than we can afford, but also because they are often loaded with hidden costs.

Credit and charge cards work by guaranteeing a merchant payment, and billing the consumer each month for purchases charged to the card. In return for this service, credit card companies charge the merchant a small percentage of the price of each item charged, and charge the consumer interest on any balance not paid in full. Some cards also charge annual fees and offer paid services.

The companies that you get your credit cards from actually have an interest in allowing you to accumulate debt. You must be very careful about what cards you choose to hold, what they charge you, and what you're getting in return. Remembering that a credit card company is looking out for itself will remind you to get all the information you need to make wise choices, and to handle the privilege of credit responsibility.

There are several kinds of cards that consumers can use to make purchases. You may be in the habit of thinking of them all as "credit cards," but in fact different cards function in different ways, and have distinct advantages and disadvantages.

CREDIT CARDS

How many credit cards should I carry in my wallet?
In my opinion, you need only one or two at most, for emergencies and convenience: to rent a car, to make a hotel reservation, or to build up a good credit rating. Two or three cards with a history of timely payments is all you need to have good credit.

All credit cards look the same to me—are they the same?
No. Visa cards and MasterCards are what are known as bank cards. All this means is that they are issued by banks or credit unions. Neither Visa nor MasterCard actually supplies the cards you carry in your wallet—banks do—but they do provide the support, the staff, and the infrastructure to the thousands of credit unions and banks that issue the cards. In exchange, the banks and credit unions have to follow the rules of these two huge financial institutions, though each bank can set its own credit standards and limits and offer whatever other advantages it wants to its customers. What's the difference between the two of them? Not a whole lot. Both are used widely, not only in this country but abroad. Both offer a lot of buying power, and most merchants accept both.

Is the Discover card a bank card, too?
Yes. The Discover card, issued by Dean Witter & Co., was brought out in the mid-1980s to compete with Visa and MasterCard. One big difference between Visa and MasterCard and the Discover card is that the Discover card can be used only in

the United States. It's also less widely accepted than Visa or MasterCard. The Discover card offers a 1 percent cash rebate program, which means it gives you 1 percent of the money you've spent back at the end of the year. (Some Visa and MasterCards offer a rebate program too—rebate programs are offered at the discretion of the issuer.) Please be aware that the Discover card company is known for computing interest in ways that end up being expensive for the card user.

CHARGE CARDS

What kind of card is American Express?
The original American Express card is not a bank card but a charge card, or a Travel and Entertainment (T&E) card. The company originally required that you pay off your entire balance in full every month. For that reason, with the first American Express card, there was neither a minimum due on your balance at the end of every month, nor interest charges, since you are not permitted to pay off your balance over time. In the '80s, the company brought out its own bank card, the Optima Card, which does allow your balance to be paid off in monthly installments, and in the late '90s, American Express brought out the Blue card. American Express cards, like Visas and MasterCards, are widely accepted, though sometimes merchants who accept bank cards don't accept American Express. This is because American Express charges merchants a higher fee for the "privilege" of accepting their cards. This promotes the notion of American Express card membership—that by carrying or honoring it you have somehow become a member of their "club." This is just good marketing talking.

What are the advantages and disadvantages of the American Express card?

One major disadvantage of the American Express card is that in 1999 the company instituted what is known as a no sue clause. This means that when you sign up for an American Express card, you are signing those privileges away. The main advantage, on the other hand, is psychological: You know that if you don't pay back in full what you owe American Express at the end of each and every month, you'll be in big trouble. With the original American Express Card, you pay the full amount all at once. Certain cards the company offers also provide you with a year-end summary of all the charges made on that card by category, from restaurants to stores to hotels, which can make tax preparation every year a lot easier.

Does that mean that I can go out today and buy a $50,000 sports car with my American Express card?
No, all it means is that American Express doesn't tell you how much you can spend using its card. If your spending habits start to look out of the ordinary, you can count on getting a call from one of their service representatives, or possibly having your card frozen, until the company figures out what's going on.

Are there any other T&E cards I should know about?
Yes, Diners Club is also a T&E, or charge, card. Like its main competitor, American Express, Diners Club does not charge interest at the end of every month. Unlike American Express, Diners Club gives customers two whole billing cycles to pay off their balance in full. If they don't pay off the full amount by then, the company tacks on a relatively low 2.5 percent interest fee, and depending on the account, possibly a delinquency fee.

DEBIT CARDS

What's the difference between a credit card and a debit card?

More and more stores and supermarkets are accepting debit cards these days. Debit cards resemble credit cards, but they don't offer a line of credit, or a limit. Debit cards function like ATM cards or checks, because when you buy something with one, the money comes directly out of your account. You can spend only what you've got in your account.

What are the advantages of debit cards?

Debit cards are very convenient. With a debit card, you don't have to carry a large amount of cash, or checks. Also, debit cards may be accepted by merchants who will not accept a personal check.

Do debit cards have any disadvantages?

They certainly do. For example, when you make a purchase, the money is deducted from your account immediately, or within a couple of days, so you don't have the use of that money or earn any interest on it as you would if there were an interval between the time you made your purchase and the time you were billed. With a debit card, please note that there are no federal regulations to protect you if you have a dispute with a merchant. Also, many banks charge a fee whenever you use your debit card. I don't like this feature, but there are banks that charge no fee, so you should check around for the best deal. Be sure to ask the bank or brokerage firm if there's a monthly or annual or per-use charge for their debit cards and whether there's an additional penalty if you use the card at another bank's ATM. And then ask if there's a way to get around these various fees. Also, with a debit card, you can't stop payment on a charge you are disputing, the way you can with a check or a credit card payment. Finally, a debit card does not help you establish a credit rating.

DEPARTMENT STORE CARDS

What about department store cards?
Charge cards issued by department stores are certainly easy to get, but in the long run, they may cost you much more than they're worth. Sure, there are usually no annual fees (you should absolutely stay away from the cards that charge one), but unless you pay off your entire balance at the end of the month, the finance charges can be sky-high, as much as 20 percent or more. For some customers, the only advantage to having a department store card is to get a discount on anything purchased on the day they open an account and to receive catalogs and advance notice of special sales and discounts.

I applied for a charge card at a major department store, and they gave me a card that has both the name of the store and the name of a bank on it. What's this all about?
This is what is known as a dual card. Department stores that issue dual cards like to tell you that you have just doubled your spending power—that you can use your card both as a bank card and as an official store card. Don't buy into this. In fact, you have just taken on another credit card. Why has the department store gone into partnership with a bank? You guessed it—more profits. You might also notice that the bank is out-of-state. This is because stores that issue their own cards are held to strict state consumer regulations covering such things as interest rates and late fees. A bank that's located in another state can utterly ignore those laws.

GASOLINE CARDS

What about gasoline cards? Are they a good deal?
Gas cards, like the American Express card, are charge cards rather than bank cards, meaning customers must pay off their entire balance at the end of each month. However, in some cases, if you buy car supplies such as tires or if you use your gasoline card to pay for expensive car repairs, your gas card company will offer you revolving credit. Just like department store cards, if they allow you to carry a monthly balance, the interest can be exorbitant. Like department store cards, gas cards are typically very easy to get. They are issued by oil companies.

Sometimes when I pull into a filling station, there's a sign on the pump that says my gas will be cheaper if I pay with cash rather than with a credit card or a gas card. Is this legal?
Absolutely. Credit card company regulations do not prohibit stationowners from offering customers a discount if they pay cash. If you are asked to pay a "service fee" when you pay with a credit card or a gas card, this extra charge is known as a surcharge. Surcharges used to be illegal under federal law, but a few years ago that law was taken off the books. Most credit card companies, however, have rules against stationowners imposing surcharges, and they are still illegal in Texas, Oklahoma, Maine, Massachusetts, California, New York, Kansas, Connecticut, Colorado, and Florida.

CREDIT CARD ERRORS

I just got my credit card statement and there's a mistaken charge of $300 on it. What should I do?
I'd say that roughly 75 percent of all the people I know have stories to tell about erroneous charges on their monthly credit card statements. You should always review your monthly statements carefully. Here are some of the things you may find:

- Your statement lists a charge you don't recognize and certainly didn't make.
- Your statement shows a charge for theater tickets or airplane tickets that you didn't receive.
- You returned an item to a store but it's not reflected on the statement.
- You didn't receive your statement one month—even though it's been delivered to the same address for years—and suddenly you're being charged a delinquency fee or finance charge for failing to make a payment.

If one of these errors, or any other, appears on your credit card statement, by law you are permitted to withhold payment on the particular charge.

Should I call up my credit card company first and tell them?
Yes—but then you need to put it in writing. In this instance, it's the law. The Fair Credit Billing Act (FCBA) says that all inquiries about billing errors must be made in writing, no later

than 60 days from the date of the mistaken or disputed charge, or from the date your faulty credit card statement was mailed to you—not the date you received it. Your letter to the credit card company should contain all pertinent identifying information, including your name, your address, and your account number, as well as a full description of the error in question—what date it took place and the reasons why you think the charge is not correct.

Last month there was a charge on my credit card bill that I didn't make. I wrote my credit card company a letter and sent it to the address where I send my minimum balance, but they claim they never got it. I forgot to keep a copy of my letter.

Always, *always* keep a copy of any correspondence you send to any financial institution, whether a bank, a credit union, or a credit card company. Your letter should be typed or word-processed, not written by hand. Send your letter by certified mail, return receipt requested, and make sure you send it to the proper address, which is usually different from the address to which you send your payments every month. (Remember, this is a billing inquiry, not a payment, and you don't want your letter to get lost in the shuffle.) You will often see a phone number and address specifically for billing inquiries on your statement itself.

If I'm disputing a charge on my credit card statement, can I wait until it's settled to pay my bill in full?

According to FCBA rules and regulations, you are not obliged to pay any charge you are questioning—or, for that matter, any interest on that charge. But this does not mean that you can withhold payment for the rest of your bill. Once you've written a letter questioning the charge, you can sit back and allow the credit card company with its enormous resources to conduct a proper and thorough investigation. Most mistaken charge cases are usually handled fairly quickly and painlessly. But be sure to pay the other charges. Otherwise, you'll be racking up penalties and interest charges, and have no recourse to challenge them.

My credit card company says that I have to prove that the charge I'm disputing is wrong, but I have no way to do this. What should I do?
Your credit card company is in error. It is not the consumer's responsibility to prove there was a billing error. The credit card company has two billing cycles, or 90 days, whichever comes first, to resolve your problem, which usually happens in one of two ways: Either the company agrees that the charge was incorrect and credits your account accordingly, or you will receive a letter telling you that the charge was correct along with an explanation of why it was.

If I don't pay the charge that I am questioning, will this show up on my credit report as a late payment?
No, it will not. Disputed charges do not count as late payments and are not reported to any credit bureaus.

What if after doing an investigation, the credit card company says that the charge that I'm disputing is correct, but I still disagree. Do I have any way to appeal their decision?
If you believe that the credit card company is still in the wrong and that the charge is unfair or mistaken, you have a couple of options. You can either pay the disputed amount (plus all interest charges) or continue to withhold payment from the card company. If you choose the latter option, you must inform the

credit card company of your decision—again, not by calling but in writing, via certified mail, return receipt requested, and making sure that you keep a copy of the letter. At this point, the card company has two options of its own: It can try to get you to pay up, or it can report your account as delinquent, though if it does that, it must inform the credit bureau that the reason for nonpayment is a disputed charge.

What if I discover a mistake on my credit card statement more than two months after my statement was issued?
You can still go ahead and dispute the charge in writing, but it might cost you some money. Call your credit card issuer and find out what their regulations say. If the cost of investigation exceeds the amount of the charge that you believe is mistaken, you might want to think twice about disputing the charge.

STOPPING PAYMENT

How do I go about stopping payment on an item I bought that was defective?
The ability to stop payment is one of the best protections that credit cards offer. There are, however, some important rules and guidelines that have to be followed. You can use your stop-payment privilege only if the defective item cost more than $50. The purchase generally has to have been made within 100 miles of your billing address (though there are exceptions to this rule; inquire with your credit card company). Before you seek to stop payment, you have to have made a genuine effort to resolve the problem you are having with the item, or the service, with the company that provided it. And you can only

stop payment on amounts for which you have not yet paid the credit card company.

What happens when I do stop payment? Will the merchant give me back my money?
The amount will be credited to your account.

What if I bought an air conditioner and it broke down a month after I bought it, but the store refuses to give me a refund?
You can still use your stop-payment feature. You must notify your credit card company within 60 days of the date the card company sent you the statement containing the disputed item. Please remember that the 60 days are counted from the date that they send you the statement, *not* the date you receive it. The 60-day rule covers, among other things, erroneous charges for items you refuse because you did not order them, deliveries to the wrong address, and late deliveries.

CANCELING A CREDIT CARD

How do I cancel my credit card?
If you want to cancel your credit card and close your account, you must inform the credit card company in writing. Send your letter to their billing inquiries address. Again, make sure you keep a copy of the letter, and send the original via certified mail, return receipt requested. (If you are paying off your balance at the same time, also keep a copy of your check. Send the check to the payment address, as usual, or to the customer service center.) If you do not want to use a particular credit card anymore, don't make the mistake of sticking it in your dresser

drawer and forgetting about it. If you do this, the credit bureau will assume that the card account is still open, and its activity (annual fees and recurring subscription charges, for example) will continue to appear on your credit report, which may make it harder for you to qualify for a new credit card at a lower rate. Not to mention that you run the risk of someone else abusing your card.

Should I keep my credit card statements, or can I throw them in the trash?

Keep *all* financial records—canceled checks, bank statements, credit card statements, any other account bills—for at least six years. This is the IRS's legal statute of limitations on audits.

I was given a corporate American Express card for business purposes. I left my job before my company reimbursed me for some of these expenses. Am I liable for these charges, or is my old employer liable?

You are probably liable for these charges, particularly if your former employer is disputing any of them. It all depends on the agreement you made with your company when they opened a corporate account for you. In some cases, the employer is liable for outstanding debts, in other cases, the employee is liable, and in still others, both of you are liable. To find out who is responsible for your charges, call AmEx and ask for a customer service representative, and/or check with your former employer's human resource department.

STOLEN OR LOST DEBIT/CREDIT CARDS

If someone steals my debit card and somehow knows my PIN, can they empty out my account or is there any sort of protection against this?

Unfortunately, there isn't. The problem with a PIN is that a bank machine can't identify you as the true owner of the card. All it knows is that the correct PIN was entered. If someone finds out your PIN, it could mean big trouble.

Won't the bank limit my liability?

The bank will not hold you liable for more than $50 if—and this is a big if—you notify the card issuer within two business days of discovering that your card is missing. (Some banks and credit card companies will contact you if they see unusual activity on the card.) If your card is stolen or missing call the bank immediately. Follow up this call with a written notice sent by registered mail, and keep a copy for your records. If you wait longer than two days, however, but act before 60 days to notify the card issuer, you will be liable for the first $500. Longer than 60 days, you will be responsible for all withdrawals until you inform them.

How long does the card company have to replace the money that was taken out of my account?

The issuer has up to 20 days to credit your account after you have notified them.

What about my ATM receipts? Do they contain any information that could help a thief?

Always take your ATM receipt with you, even if you just take it home and destroy it. In some cases, your entire account number is printed on that receipt, and if a smart thief knew your account number and somehow got your card and your PIN, you would be sunk.

What if I lose my credit card or it gets stolen?

Report any lost or stolen credit cards to your credit card company immediately and follow it up with written notice, as described above. It's a good idea to check your cards every now and then, to make sure they are all in place. Write down the account numbers of all your cards, and put them in a secret place in your house, and/or in your safe deposit box, if you have one.

CREDIT CARDS AND SECURITY

A friend told me it's not safe to sign my name on the back of my credit card. Do you agree?

I disagree. You should sign the back of your credit card to protect yourself from unauthorized charges. You sign your name on the back of a credit card so a merchant can compare that signature with the one on his receipt. What if your cards are unsigned and your wallet is lost or stolen? Whoever finds it or stole it could sign his name to the back of your card and use it to rack up hundreds of dollars or more in purchases. It's not foolproof, but signing your name on your card makes it just that bit more difficult for someone to take advantage of you.

How can I prevent somebody from using my card?

You can do a number of different things to ensure that your card and/or your account number don't end up in the wrong hands. For example, never, under any circumstances, give out your account number or any other personal information over the phone unless you are utterly positive that the caller represents a legitimate business. If you are in any doubt, ask them for their phone number, and call them back. Even better, ask them to send you information in the mail. As a general rule, I would not give my credit card number to anyone whom I had not called.

What about giving my credit card number to an online company?

There have been so many advances recently in encryption software that make the transmission of sensitive, confidential information over the Internet safer than ever before. I wouldn't be concerned about giving out credit card information to reputable online merchants who have a totally secured website. In my opinion, it could be more dangerous to sign a credit card slip at a store or restaurant where they have not only your name and number, but your signature as well.

Are there any specific credit card scams on the World Wide Web that I should be aware of?

I would be very suspicious of any e-mails claiming to be from your service provider and asking you to resubmit your credit card number. If this ever happens, call your service provider at once to verify that the e-mail came from them. Consumers have also gotten ripped off by websites that say they are the official home pages of well-known companies. A consumer gives out a credit card number in exchange for merchandise, and the merchandise never arrives. But the con artist behind the fake web page now has the consumer's credit card number!

How else can I take precautions, either on the computer or in real life?

Just as you would never tell anybody your credit card account number, you should never tell anybody your PIN. Remember, do not write it on your card in any form, even in code, or carry it in your wallet. Never give it to anybody over the phone. Try to avoid obvious PINs, such as your birthdate. If a thief stole your wallet, he could easily find your birthdate on your driver's license.

FINDING THE BEST CREDIT CARD OFFER

DECIPHERING CREDIT CARD OFFERS

Many credit card solicitations that I get in the mail offer a "low introductory rate." Is this on the level?

Yes and no. Again, scrutinize these offers very carefully—sometimes when introductory rates are lower, the rates for balance transfers and cash advances are higher, or the low introductory rate may jump by 10 percent or more after a few months. Obviously, you want the card with the lowest introductory rate, and the longer the low rate lasts, the better. In any case, if you have good credit you never want a card whose normal rate is above 11 percent.

Under "annual fees" on my credit card application, there's a zero. Do I lose out on any advantages if I don't pay the card company an annual fee?

No. In fact, a credit card, in my opinion, should have no annual fee. If it does, take your business elsewhere.

Why do I get so many offers for credit cards from banks located in either the Midwest or Delaware?

Some states have friendlier laws than others when it comes to lending money to consumers—friendlier to the card issuers, that is. Out-of-state banks are not necessarily subject to the consumer protection statutes of your home state! Suppose you send in your monthly payment late, and according to the laws of your state, you are liable only for a limited amount, say, $10? Your issuing bank in South Dakota can charge you two or three times that amount if it's permitted by law in that state! You should be on the lookout for cards from issuers in states that offer the best consumer protection.

FIGURING OUT THE ANNUAL PERCENTAGE RATE (APR)

What is the annual percentage rate?

The APR, or annual percentage rate, is the interest, or the commission, that you are paying to the credit card company for the use of their money. This is the fee that will be levied against your account if you fail to pay off the complete amount at the end of every month. You might see this rate listed either as an APR or as a monthly periodic rate. If your annual percentage rate is, say, 15.9 percent, you will have paid a 15.9 percent interest fee on outstanding charges for that year's purchases. To find out your monthly periodic rate, divide your APR by 12 (the number of months in a year). Sometimes companies just quote and charge a monthly rate; if this is the case, multiply that monthly percentage rate by 12 to see what your annual rate will be on any outstanding balance you might be carrying by year's end. Please note that depending on how the credit card company calculates its interest charges, the amount of your payments could be higher than you calculated.

How do credit card companies calculate interest charges?

There are two ways credit card companies compute interest, and only one of these ways benefits you. The first way—and the better way for consumers—is for the card companies to charge you interest on your average daily balance, including new purchases. Let's say you charge $1,000 on your credit card for a CD player. When your credit card statement comes in, you're short on cash so you pay $500 against your $1,000 balance. When you get your next credit card statement, you will owe interest only on the remaining $500 that you did not pay the month before.

The second way credit card companies calculate interest is by means of what is called the two-cycle average daily balance, including new purchases. Take that same $1,000 balance, of which you paid off $500. If your credit card company uses the two-month average daily balance method of calculating interest charges, your next month's statement will show that you owe the credit card company interest on almost the entire $1,000, even though you paid off $500 of it the month before. Why? Because if you do not pay off the balance in full, the credit card company charges you interest on the average daily balance over two months, or two billing cycles, not just one.

THE FINE PRINT

There seem to be so many things to consider when applying for a credit card. What exactly should I look for?

I've said it before, and I'll say it again: Read the fine print. Credit card companies don't really expect you to read the text they've tucked away in lower left-hand corners or inside boxes. They assume you're too lazy, or indifferent, or that even if you're not, the information will be in language you don't understand. Don't let them get away with this. When you receive a credit card offer, go immediately to the small print in the so-called Schumer Box.

What is the Schumer Box?

When Congress passed the Fair Credit and Charge Card Disclosure Act of 1989 (which is a part of the Truth-in-Lending Act), one of its new laws was that all costs associated with a credit card must be featured prominently on the application or on the offer itself. These costs must also be easy to read—and without a magnifying glass. The box in which these charges are displayed is known informally as the Schumer Box, named after Democratic Representative Charles Schumer of New York, who helped push the Fair Credit and Charge Card Disclosure Act through Congress. The Schumer Box contains information that you should consider carefully before you decide to apply for any credit card. First, you should take a look at a credit card's APR, or annual percentage rate.

GRACE PERIOD

My credit card application mentions a "grace period." What is this?

The grace period is the time between the closing date of your billing cycle and the date you have to pay your balance in full. No interest is charged during this period. However, with a few exceptions, this grace period applies only if you are not carrying an account balance. If you are carrying a balance at the end of the month, the grace period does not apply to you. You will owe interest—starting immediately—on any new purchase you make as well as on your outstanding balance.

What else is inside the Schumer Box that I should know about?

The Schumer Box should give you information about various fees—fees for cash advances and late fees. The amount charged for the former can sometimes be higher than the fees the companies charge you when you make purchases, so be very careful with cash advances. Even if your introductory rate is 5.9 percent, and you don't owe a balance, many companies charge a flat percentage (say, 2.5 percent) on each cash advance, with a maximum fee of up to $20.

LATE FEES

What about late fees?

These can add up too if you don't pay at least your minimum balance on time, though each company's policy is different. Some will start their clock ticking if your payment is only one day late; others give you a week or two, sometimes more. Remember, the companies request that your payment be received—not postmarked—by a certain date. Remember to account for the time the mail takes, and send your payment in early.

How much are late fees, generally?

During the writing of this book (in the latter part of 1999), I called up the AT&T Universal Card Services, and a customer representative told me that for their MasterCard, a late fee of $29 is assessed the day after the date payment is due. In general, fees range from $25 to $30, which can add a hefty premium to your account!

Will my credit card payment be credited to my account the day the credit card company receives it?

Even though the Fair Credit Billing Act of 1996 requires credit card companies to credit your payment to your account on the day it is received, companies can set their own specific payment guidelines. Some companies take as many as five days to credit your account with a payment. Again, take the time to read the small print. Depending on the terms of your credit card, you might find out that you can be subject to late fees if your payment arrives even one day late.

MINIMUM PAYMENTS

What is the minimum payment I have to make on my balance every month?

Depending on your agreement with a credit card company, your minimum monthly payment will range from 1.5 percent to 4 percent of your balance. Actually, you want the figure to be higher rather than lower, because if you tend to pay just the minimum each month, the lower your required payment, the longer it will take you to pay off your debt (as credit card companies very well know). I'll say it now and I'll say it later: It's absolutely essential that you pay more than the minimum amount each month.

EXCEEDING YOUR CREDIT LIMIT

What if one month I go over my credit limit by accident?

You will be charged from $5 to $25 for "going over" your credit limit. Then you'll end up paying interest on that extra charge as well. Also, if you exceed your limit, the credit card company may have the right to change that good introductory rate you are enjoying to a significantly higher one. So there is more than one reason not to exceed your credit limit.

ANNUAL FEES

I don't carry a balance, but all of a sudden my credit card company is charging me an annual fee, which they never did before. Why?

Being a "good" customer—paying your bills on time and in full—is not what credit card companies want of you. As far as they're concerned, a "good" customer carries a lot of debt and makes interest payments over a number of months, preferably years. Most credit card companies make money in three ways: from the interest you pay; from annual fees, if applicable; and from the fees they charge merchants who accept their card. You would think this would be enough! But it's not. Some credit card companies are beginning to charge an extra fee to those responsible customers who don't carry a balance from one month to the next. Other companies charge $25 to any customers who don't pay at least $25 in interest over the course of a year.

Can credit card companies do this legally?

Yes. More and more people are defaulting on consumer loans (credit card, home equity, and car loans), so credit card companies are scrambling to think of new ways to charge you. It's your responsibility to keep on top of any changes the credit card companies make in their rules and regulations. For example, a friend of mine who usually carries a monthly balance received a notice in the mail telling him that his credit card company was changing the way they computed interest, from the average daily balance method to the two-cycle method, including new purchases. My friend didn't have to think twice—he changed cards.

SWITCHING CREDIT CARDS

How do I know if I should switch credit cards?
Remember, credit card companies are competing with one another for your business, and if you're a heavy user with a good credit history, they will make it amazingly easy for you to switch over to the card they're offering. But watch your step: Too-good-to-be-true offers are usually just that. Do your homework to make sure you really are getting the best deal out there. You may have to transfer your card balances two or three times a year to get the best deal. That's a few calls and 15 minutes of paperwork a year, and it might save you literally hundreds of dollars. When can you stop being so vigilant? When your debt is gone and you've taken the steps to guarantee it won't mount up again.

Are there any resources that will keep me informed of the best credit card offers available?
A very good way to keep up-to-date on the best credit card offers is by checking my website at *www.suzeorman.com,* in the Additional Resources section under "Best Deals for Credit Cards," or at *www.cardtrak.com* or *www.bankrate.com.* If you do not have a computer, then check a current issue of *Money* magazine or *Kiplinger's* magazine.

SILVER, GOLD, AND PLATINUM CARDS

If I get an offer to switch my regular credit card over to a silver or a gold or even a platinum one, should I go for it?

In my opinion, credit card companies count on our appetite for bigger and better, and on our never being satisfied with what we have. Maybe once upon a time, people thought that if you had a gold card you were somehow more important or richer than everybody else (maybe you thought that about yourself, too), but with the number of these cards out there these days, I doubt whether that's true anymore.

Are there any advantages to carrying a silver, gold, or platinum card?

One advantage (which I don't really think of as an advantage) is that the credit lines on Visa or MasterCard gold card usually start at around $5,000 and can reach as high as tens of thousands of dollars. (American Express cards carry no spending limits.) Also, these cards tend to offer a lot of customer perks, such as frequent flyer miles or collision-damage insurance if you use the card to pay for a rental car.

American Express gold and platinum cards send you a complete itemized annual statement at the end of the year, too, which can be helpful when you're putting your tax information together.

If I need a higher credit limit, isn't a gold or platinum card the only way to go?

Actually, if you are a big spender and you pay your bills responsibly and on time, you can maintain a balance on your regular bank card that approaches and sometimes equals the lines of credit that gold or platinum cards offer—and along the way, you can avoid paying the annual fee that some of these gold or platinum cards charge their customers for the "privilege" of carrying their card. (The American Express platinum card can be yours for $300 a year, for example.) If you spend heavily but pay off your balance every month, call up your credit card company and ask them whether your limit can be increased. If you're a responsible customer, chances are pretty good that they'll agree to this.

DELAYED PAYMENTS

I just got an offer in the mail for a credit card with "zero percent financing until Thanksgiving." This sounds fantastic! Should I go for it?
If you can in fact pay off any debt on this card by Thanksgiving, then this credit card will cost you nothing. What the credit card company is banking on, however, is that come Thanksgiving, you won't be able to pay off your balance—at which time you will probably get socked with an interest rate that compares with that of the worst department store credit cards. Before you accept this offer, be honest with yourself about whether you can pay off your debt by Thanksgiving, and be sure you know what your interest rate will be after the "zero percent financing" period is up.

CREDIT INSURANCE

I got an offer from a credit card company for credit insurance. Is this a good hedge against something terrible happening to me in the future?
Typically, credit card companies like to offer their customers four different kinds of credit insurance. Credit property insurance insures you against damage to the property that is securing your loan; credit life insurance promises you that if you die, your outstanding balance will be paid; credit disability insurance insures you against any illnesses or accidents that might cause disabilities (the companies usually provide a complete listing of which disabilities are covered); and involuntary

loss of income insurance insures against your losing your job or getting fired.

In my opinion, credit insurance isn't worth it, particularly because it is very expensive. If you want insurance, take out a general plan from a regular insurance company that covers some if not all of the same contingencies.

KEEPING TRACK OF YOUR RATES AND FEES

CHARTING INTEREST RATES

My credit card company just raised my interest rate for no apparent reason. Can they do this?
Believe it or not, they can. The expression "fixed rate" means nothing to a card company—they merely have to notify you in writing of a hike in the interest rate 15 days before it takes effect, and they're legally in the clear. Furthermore, they can then apply the new, higher interest rate to your outstanding balance. As a consumer dealing with credit card companies, you're usually in the position of "take it or leave it." Sure, you can lodge a complaint against the card company, but this is often an expensive, laborious process: You have to go through a procedure known as arbitration, which could end up costing you more than it would be worth.

What's the actual monetary difference between a high-interest-rate card and a low-interest-rate card?
Look at the table below and you will see how much more and how much longer you will pay with higher interest rates. For

example, if you have a $4,000 credit card balance and are paying a minimum of $100 every month:

At this interest rate	It will take you this long to pay off your credit card debt	And you'll pay this much in interest
5.9 percent	45 months	$ 465
7.9 percent	47 months	$ 658
9.9 percent	49 months	$ 874
12.9 percent	53 months	$1,257
15.9 percent	58 months	$1,736
18.9 percent	63 months	$2,362

PRE-APPROVED CARDS

Several times a month a credit card offer shows up in my mail, saying I am pre-approved for this or that card. Can you explain pre-approval?
"Congratulations, Suze Orman, you're pre-approved!" All of us have this experience, but what does this mean? Not very much, unfortunately. All "pre-approved" really means is that you have passed an initial screening. What it doesn't mean is that you are suddenly eligible for a $10,000, $15,000, or $25,000 line of credit.

What do credit card companies base their pre-approval on?
Pre-approval is based on your income level, what other cards you carry, and whether you have a history of paying your credit card balances responsibly and on time.

Why can't credit card companies commit to their "pre-approved" offer?

They're being cautious. A lot of bad things could potentially happen to you between the time you fill out the application and send it back to the credit card company and when they process it. For example, you could declare bankruptcy. Or, as we saw earlier, you could apply for five new credit cards at the same time (remember, this is a red flag for the credit bureaus, who take this to mean you're about to go on a charging spree). Or you could lose your job or your house. The credit card companies know this, which is why they slip a provision that allows them to deny your application. (Of course, it's in much smaller print than "Congratulations, You're Pre-approved.")

GETTING OFF THOSE CREDIT CARD MAILING LISTS

How do credit card companies get my name and address? Does a credit bureau sell it to them? How can I get off these lists?

If credit bureaus already have an active file on you, it's probably too late to get your name taken off these solicitation lists. The only way to keep yourself off a list? Pay cash for absolutely everything. Don't give your name or address to any department or retail stores, and don't shop by mail. And don't ever apply for a job or insurance. As you can see, keeping your name off credit card mailing lists is virtually impossible.

Aren't there companies you can write to in order to have your name removed from solicitation lists?

Yes. There is a way to remove your name from some if not all of these lists. Contact one of the big-three credit bureaus (see the Additional Resources section at the back of this book for their addresses, phone numbers, and websites) and request a form for removing your name from lists for unsolicited credit and insurance offers. You can also contact the Direct Marketing Association's Mail and Telephone Preference Services (again, see the Additional Resources section).

CREDIT CARD DEBT
AND RELATIONSHIPS

I owe my sister $5,000, and every time I see her I think about it, though she doesn't mention it. I also owe $8,000 on my credit cards. Since the credit card companies are charging me interest, is it okay for me to pay off my credit card debt before I pay back my sister?

No, I don't think so. I've seen money damage personal relationships more times than you can imagine, and though there are times when helping out a family member or friend is absolutely the right thing to do, it should always be taken very seriously—for it is a serious matter. Whether it's personal or institutional, debt is debt. Even if your sister has loaned you the money indefinitely, it doesn't mean you should not be paying her anything on this loan. If you pay her just $25 a month, you will feel better about yourself. Remember, self-esteem is a key factor in dealing with debt. The fact that you think about the money you owe your sister every time you two get together is a sign that this debt is affecting your relationship.

My wife has just admitted to me that she has been secretly hiding $3,000 worth of debt on a credit card I didn't know anything about. What should I do?

Although your initial reaction to your wife's disclosure may be anger or disappointment, please realize that she has taken the first, difficult step toward freeing herself—and you—from debt. Think about why your wife might have been reluctant to tell you about her debt. Could it be a symptom of more fundamental problems of trust and support in your relationship? Please know that you and your wife are not alone. Secret debt is not uncommon, whether it's a spouse's Visa bill with a growing balance, or the department store bill that never seems to go down, or the blank check so thoughtfully provided by the Optima company that you wrote out, deposited, and haven't been able to pay off. Every little charge adds up, until it's too late and too embarrassing to tell anybody.

If you are hiding debt of any kind, I urge you to tell your partner. Debt can't be kept secret forever, and your integrity, your self-respect, and your relationship are more important than your partner's reaction. Your debt is your partner's burden and responsibility, too. Don't keep him or her in the dark. Together, you can work to free yourself from debt.

If I'm married, am I responsible for money my husband owes on credit cards that are in his name alone, and vice versa?

Personally, I believe that if you are married, you have pledged your support and responsibility—emotional and financial—to your spouse. Legally, the answer to this question depends on which state you live in. In many states, you are responsible for your spouse's debt whether or not your name is on the account. For instance, in California if your husband goes out the day after you are married and gets a Visa card, charges $5,000 on it, and then cannot pay for it, guess who is also liable? You are. Be aware that you and your spouse having credit cards in your own names does not necessarily mean you are not responsible for each other's debt.

My wife and I separated recently. Can I legally keep her from using our joint credit cards?

If either you or your wife tells the credit card company that you want to close your joint account, the creditor should close the account. (In that event, neither of you can use the account, but you both are responsible for the full balance that you accumulated before you closed it.) First call the credit card company and ask them to close your account, and then follow up with a letter. As always, send your letter via certified mail, return receipt requested, and keep a copy for your records. If for some reason the credit card company is not cooperative when you call them, go ahead and send your letter anyway, and send a copy to the bank's compliance officer. He or she is responsible for making sure the bank complies with federal credit laws. Not only will this action get your message across, but if this matter ever went to court, you would have left behind a paper trail that would serve as evidence that you're not responsible for any credit card debt incurred by your separated (or ex) spouse subsequent to your request that the account be closed.

My wife and I recently got a divorce, but she continues to use our joint credit card to make purchases. Am I responsible for paying those bills?

Unfortunately, as far as your creditors are concerned, you are responsible for those bills—unless you have notified them that you want to close the account.

Between us, my wife and I have a number of credit cards, most of which we never use. My wife says we should get rid of the cards we don't use; I think we should keep them in case of an emergency. Who's right?
Your wife is. Having many credit cards, whether you use them or not, could actually look bad on your credit report, and if you applied for a lower-interest-rate card, you could be turned down. Why? Because you have so much credit available to you, credit card companies assume you could rack up a lot of debt in a hurry, which makes you a poor risk. You should call the credit card companies in question and close the accounts you are not using. Just keep one card in case of an emergency.

My aunt has offered to help me get out of credit card debt by lending me $15,000 at a very low interest rate. Do you think this is a good idea?
Borrowing money from your aunt, or any relative or friend, can sound like a good idea—but you should be prepared for the possibility that it may backfire. Is a low- or no-interest-rate loan really worth risking your relationship? And will the loan really teach you the lesson of getting yourself out of debt—and *staying* out of debt? In my experience, too often emergency bail-outs only reset the clock for people prone to debt—and before they know it, they've racked up a whole new set of charges and are right back where they were before their loved one helped them out.

I understand what you're saying but my aunt and I have talked about this, and know that the loan should be treated like the serious business it is. Do you have any advice about how we should proceed?
If you do decide to borrow money from a relative or friend, keep things as businesslike as possible. For example, I think

that it's only fair that you pay your aunt an interest rate above what she could earn in a savings or money market fund. You should be very clear about the amount of debt you are carrying and if possible, you should sign a contract that spells out the terms of the loan. Otherwise, it can be too tempting not to take your aunt's loan as seriously as you should, and too tempting to take on new debt.

I have a friend who borrowed money from her father. Last week her father forgave her the loan and said she didn't have to pay him back. Are there any problems with this?

On the face of it, your friend seems to be a girl who caught a lucky break. But she should know this much: If a friend or relative who has loaned you money someday decides to cancel that loan, the IRS will consider the money that you received from your friend or relative taxable income. How will the IRS ever find out, you may wonder? They can spot an unusual increase—or decrease—in bank statements during an audit or via a red-flag system. Both gifts-givers and recipients should clear all the tax implications with a good accountant.

When my parents die and their estate is settled, will I be responsible for whatever credit card debt they have?

You're not personally responsible for your deceased parents' credit card debt unless your name is on the account. If there is no money in the estate to pay the debt, most credit card companies write off the debt owed by the deceased.

My husband died recently, and I am wondering how his death will affect my credit and account.

This is one of the reasons why I advise couples to have joint and individual credit card accounts. If only one partner worked and then was to die, the stay-at-home partner might have trouble getting a card in his or her own name without a steady income to support the credit card application. So please do not wait until you find yourself in this situation. In the case of the recent widow in the above question, I would say, if your accounts were held jointly and you are certain that you can maintain the account on your own, then by all means go ahead and tell the creditors that the account will now be in your name only. It might also be a good idea to inform the three credit bureaus that your husband has died, otherwise you may find that other credit card companies continue to solicit him in the mail. (You can write to the credit bureaus at the addresses listed in the Additional Resources section.)

CHILDREN AND CREDIT CARDS

I have two children, ages 10 and 13. What's the best way for me to start educating them about credit cards and about debt in general?

I believe it's never too soon to start your children's financial education. Think of the message you're sending your children when you pull out your Visa card to pay for gas or a meal at your favorite restaurant. Because you've simply scribbled your name on a little piece of paper and no money has changed hands, your kids might assume the gas or the meal was free! Explain how these cards work—that the credit card issuer is allowing you to use their money and that you have promised to pay them back at the end of the month. Also explain that the credit card issuer charges you to use their money, and that they will continue to charge you until you repay them, which is how you can get into trouble.

My son, a college sophomore, has gotten himself in trouble with credit cards and owes money to the tune of nearly $3,000. I'm absolutely floored, especially since he's on financial aid! How can credit card companies encourage 20-year-olds to spend money they don't have?

The answer is pretty easy. I'm not saying that your son is an innocent victim, but credit card companies make it fairly simple for college students to get themselves in over their heads in debt. Why do credit card companies target our relatively financially inexperienced sons and daughters? Many college kids, away from home for the first time, like the grown-up feeling that credit cards can give them. And the credit card companies know that if they can get a customer early, that customer will most likely remain loyal to—or dependent on—their product for a very long time.

Don't people who apply for a credit card need to show evidence that they are earning a living?

College students often don't need to show an income, or even get their application cosigned by a parent or other responsible adult, to get a credit card sent to them. Card companies assume that if college students get into trouble, their parents will be there to bail them out.

Is it a good or a bad idea for a college student to have a credit card?

Despite the potential pitfalls, I think it's a good idea for college students to have one credit card, since the older they get, the harder it may be for them to qualify for a credit card and to establish credit, particularly if they take their time finding a job once they've graduated.

The card and charging privileges, however, should come

with some strict guidelines. For example, there should be a credit limit of $500 or $1,000 at most. Also, a duplicate statement should be sent directly to the parents. In this case I'd stay away from American Express cards, because the annual fee is relatively high and the card has no spending limit.

My daughter is going to college next month, and she's taking her first credit card with her. What should I tell her?

Set a limit on your daughter's spending. For example, tell her that her credit card can be used only for certain kinds of purchases (e.g., for airplane tickets to travel between school and home) or in emergencies. Then make sure you define emergency! Make sure she also knows your position about bailing her out if she runs up an amount of debt that she finds herself unable to pay—and don't budge from that position. Explain credit ratings to her, and that her credit card is a way for her to establish a good credit rating for the long haul. Remind her that if she pays her bills late, this will show up on her credit report and could affect her purchasing power later in life.

My daughter is in college. Am I legally responsible for her credit card bills if for some reason she can't pay them?

If your name is not on the credit card application, then no, you are not responsible for your daughter's debt. She will have to deal with collection agencies by herself! However, if you cosigned her application, then you are responsible for the balance owed.

My son took my Visa card to the mall and came back with $100 in video games. When my credit card statement came, I refused to pay the video store bill, since in

my opinion, I did not authorize my son to buy video games! The bank says that since it is my account, I have to pay up. Do I?

First of all, your son should never take credit cards or cash from you without your explicit permission. This is dangerous, irresponsible behavior that can cause serious problems for your son later in life. I know—I used to take money from my father's pants pockets at night and as an adult I ended up tens of thousands of dollars in debt. I'm not suggesting there's a direct link between these two states, but it tells me that you and your son need to have a talk about money and responsibility now, before the problem gets any bigger.

Now, for the sake of learning from this example, I'm going to assume you gave your son permission to use your card—perhaps you even got him his own card on your account, which he was only to use to make purchases you authorized in advance. Even if this was the case, you are nevertheless responsible for the charges on the card. The Truth-in-Lending Act defines "unauthorized use" as the use of a credit card by a person who does not have the authority to use that card. As far as the bank is concerned, you gave your son implicit consent to use the card however he wished. Some courts may disagree, but do you really want to take it that far?

The fact of the matter is that someone—not the bank—is going to have to pay that $100 video-store bill. It will either be you or your son. I vote for your son. If he can't pay up immediately, make him return the videos or tell him that he owes you $100, which he can pay back on a schedule the two of you work out.

My 40-year-old son charged $3,000 on his credit card, and now, four months later, he has not made a single payment to the company. The company has been leav-

ing a lot of messages. One of these messages told him he could pay off the entire debt by paying 50 percent of what he owed. Is this a good idea?

The credit card company is trying to cut their losses by offering your son a settlement. This may seem like an easy way out. But if your son accepts the settlement offer, it could affect his ability to get credit in the future.

If your son pays 50 percent of his outstanding balance, or $1,500, his credit report will say that the account is now "settled in full." But the credit report also will show a balance remaining on the account—the $1,500 your son did not pay—as well as a note of this settlement. This flag will remain on his credit report for seven years. Is it worth it? No. He should pay back as much as he can afford every month until the debt is paid off. Encourage your son to call the Consumer Credit Counseling Service and take this reckless situation in hand.

The holidays are fast approaching, and I'm starting to feel that typical end-of-the-year anxiety, mostly about the bills that'll come swarming in after the new year. Any suggestions on how to rein in my spending?

Everybody knows the holidays can be one of the most tempting times of the year to overindulge—in food, in drink, and in credit card use. The holidays are also a time when your generosity can overwhelm your common sense, so my advice (as always) is to be very, very conscious of what you spend money on. Try to plan ahead and get your Christmas shopping done early, during the non-holiday months and especially during sales. Also figure out, *before* you hit the stores, how much you want to spend on each of your loved ones, and then make it a point not to go over that figure. If you are shopping in a department store, try only to use cash, and don't charge anything. Even if you want to "spread the wealth" among your various credit cards, remember the interest on department store cards is usually sky-high. Finally, I urge you to think of gifts that have lasting meaning. The sad truth is that most of us cannot remember what gifts we got the year before—no matter how much they cost. Thoughtful, personalized presents are not necessarily the most expensive ones.

Last year around the holidays, my credit card company sent me a pack of "convenience checks." Should I use them?

Use these so-called convenience checks only if you are prepared to pay exorbitant interest rates. Find out what the interest rate is, and if you don't like it, tear the checks up. These checks are usually "convenient" only for the card companies.

RENTAL CARS

If I rent a car using my credit card, do I need to pay for additional insurance?

Some, but not all, credit card companies provide collision-damage insurance on rental cars. Instead of paying $10 or $15 a day extra on your rental car bill, you get this feature automatically when you use your credit card to pay for the rental car. This insurance is usually available with gold and platinum cards, but check your regular credit card, too—it may offer the same insurance. In any case, coverage via AAA may be the most sensible and affordable option.

What exactly does this rental-car collision-damage insurance cover?

If your credit card offers you collision-damage insurance and you get into an accident with your rental car, your credit card company will pay the difference between what your regular automobile insurer pays and the total cost of the damage. Before you see a penny from the credit card company, you must file a claim with your own insurance company. This is known as secondary coverage. Diners Club, however, offers consumers primary coverage. This means that if you get into a fender-bender in your rental car, Diners Club will pay the car rental company for the damage—before you go to your insurance company.

CREDIT BUREAUS / CREDIT REPORTS

What exactly is a credit rating?

A credit rating is a numbered system called the "credit scoring system" that informs a variety of lenders and issuers of credit—mortgage companies, credit card companies, department stores, landlords, etc.—how timely and responsible you have been with your various creditors. Since the rating system is essentially universal, it is easy for potential lenders, employers, or landlords to determine your credit worthiness and assess whether you are a good or bad risk when they are considering entering into a financial or working arrangement with you.

Can I see my credit report? If so, how do I get a copy of it?

At your request, a credit bureau must give you the information in your file—and a list of everyone who has requested it recently. If you have been turned down for a credit card because of information supplied by the credit bureau, there is no charge for the report if you request it within 60 days of receiving notice of the action. You can apply for this through the credit card company that turned you down.

You also are entitled to one free report every 12 months upon request if you certify that:

- you are unemployed and plan to seek employment within 60 days;
- you are on welfare; or
- your report is inaccurate due to fraud.

Under any other circumstances, a credit bureau may charge you up to $8 (depending on where you live) for a copy of your report.

I was just denied a lower-interest credit card, with no explanation. Where did they find out the information about my financial history?

Credit card companies, banks, mortgage lenders, and credit unions purchase information about you through credit bureaus. Credit bureaus—also known as credit repackaging agencies—make a terrific living through amassing data about your financial life, putting it all together, and when the time comes, making it available to lenders, employers, landlords, insurers, and other businesses.

How many credit bureaus are in this country? And how do I know which one has my file?

There are numerous credit bureaus in the United States, but in most cases, you'll be dealing with one that's associated with one of the big three major credit bureau companies: Experian (formerly TRW Information Systems, Inc., headquartered in Orange, California); Trans Union (based in Chicago, Illinois); and Equifax (formerly CBI/Equifax, based in Atlanta, Georgia).

What's in my credit file?

First of all, there are two different kinds of credit files: standard and investigative. Unless you're a fugitive or being investigated by some high-stakes company, you probably have a standard credit file. A standard credit file notes your name, address, date of birth, past addresses (home and work), Social Security number, phone numbers, and the name of your spouse and/or ex-spouses, if applicable. It contains a reasonably complete and up-to-date outline of your financial history, including your employment history, your marriages and divorces, your liens, your bankruptcy information, and, most important, your credit history. It will list the names of your creditors—including retailers, card issuers, and other lenders—and your payment history on these accounts for the previous 24 to 60 months, including your credit limits and current balances. Did someone sue you in court and win? It'll be in your credit file. Do you owe child support? It'll be in your credit file. Your standard credit file also contains an extensive list of your credit accounts, often known as a tradeline by the employees of the credit bureau.

What's in my tradeline?

The tradeline includes such information as when you opened these credit accounts, how much outstanding debt you have, whether an account is in your name only or is a joint account, and any negative information connected to the accounts, such as bankruptcy or a history of late payments. Some people may find it scary to think that someone is keeping such close tabs on them, but not much borrowing or lending would take place without credit reports.

How did the credit bureau get all this information about me?

When you applied for your first credit card, whoever was processing your application probably tried to find out your financial history, and since you didn't have one (at least as far as the credit bureau was concerned), your credit report got started. Credit bureaus go to every entity out there to collect and organize information about an individual's credit and payment habits. This information is available to those with a legal permissible purpose to see it in the form of a credit report. The credit bureaus then sell this information to those requesting a report—which is how they make their money. Basically, it's their business to find out as much as they can about your financial history.

How often is my credit report updated?

The truth is, your credit report essentially doesn't exist until someone asks for it. When a bank or an insurance company or a credit card company calls up the credit bureau and asks them for a copy of your credit report, the credit bureau puts all the information together. Then they present it to the lender, often via computer, as your "report."

What criteria do creditors use when they are deciding whether or not to extend me credit?

The three guidelines that a lot of creditors use when they are deciding whether or not to extend you credit are sometimes known as the Three C's of good credit. They are character, capacity, and collateral.

What do they mean by "character"?

From the point of view of credit bureaus, character doesn't mean you're a good person who does charity work in your spare time. When used by credit bureaus, character refers to whether or not you are trustworthy as far as advancing credit is concerned—i.e., do you pay your bills on time?

What does "capacity" mean?

As used by the credit bureaus, capacity refers to your financial position. For example: Are you earning enough income to be able to consistently pay interest charges? Do you have an alternate source of income, such as money left to you by your family or an investment portfolio, that you could draw on in an emergency?

What does "collateral" mean?

Collateral is the security that the lender needs in order to advance you the credit, or the loan. It can be a house, or a car, or stock certificates. If you default on your loan, depending on its type, your lender may take possession of your collateral.

None of these things really says much about me as a person, does it?

Of course not! "Character" in particular may not accurately reflect your ability to pay back a loan. Nonetheless, these are the criteria credit bureaus and lenders use.

After taking these three things into consideration, how does the credit card company decide whether to accept me or turn me down?

After they evaluate the Three C's, lenders use two more criteria to decide whether your application—for a credit card, for a home equity loan, for a mortgage—should be approved or turned down without explanation: judgmental evaluation and credit scoring.

What is judgmental evaluation?

In a judgmental evaluation, someone from the bank or the credit card company takes a long, hard look at your credit history. At the same time, he or she will take into consideration certain things about you that a credit report might not reflect; in some cases, lenders may even use such unscientific methods as their gut feelings. This bank representative decides whether or not your application should be approved. Judgmental evaluation used to be much more common, but nowadays it is being replaced more and more by credit scoring.

What is credit scoring?

Credit scoring is a way the bank or the credit card company tries to predict, as best they can, how risky it might be to lend money to you, whether in the form of a loan or credit.

When your application arrives at the bank or the credit card company, an employee enters all the pertinent information from your application into the company computer. He or she is looking for any red flags, such as: Have you ever filed for bankruptcy? Do you owe child support payments? If you pass this human screening, technology takes over. The company's computer dials up the credit bureau's computer, which assembles your credit report on the spot. The computer (not an actual human being) analyzes the data on your application and in your credit report, and "decides" whether or not you are a person worth granting a loan or extending credit to.

What is the computer looking for?

It is "looking" to see whether or not you have data in common with other customers who pay their bills on time and are considered trustworthy. It's more complicated, of course—it can get very mathematical—but that's the basic idea.

I keep hearing the term FICO in reference to my credit score. What is it?

FICO—short for Fair Isaac Company, which created it—is a credit scoring system that many credit card companies use when they are evaluating the various risks associated with lending you money. A lot of other mathematical models used by credit card companies do the same thing as FICO, but no matter what they are, their results tend to be referred to as FICO scores.

What are the components of a consumer's FICO score?

FICO scores are numbers that the credit bureaus generate based on information about your checking and savings accounts, any outstanding debt you may have, and your payment record. The better your credit, the higher your FICO score; the worse your credit, the lower your FICO score. Scores range from 350 to 900. You want a FICO score of 620 or higher. If your score is anywhere below that, you are considered enough of a risk for default that most companies won't take a chance on you. If your score falls between 620 and 650, you will stay in a kind of limbo until you have provided the lender with further documentation. If your score over 650, you're in the money.

What could lower my FICO score?

The same things that damage a credit report will lower your FICO score: bankruptcy, a history of late payments on various accounts, too many credit cards that you have maxed out, or too skimpy a credit history. Even numerous credit report inquiries can lower your score.

If I've been denied credit, can the credit bureau tell me why?

You are entitled to receive a free copy of your credit file from the bureau that supplied the information to your prospective lender within 60 days of being denied credit. I recommend that you check your credit status from time to time anyway, in order to make sure that it is completely accurate.

What are my rights with credit bureaus? Are there some things credit bureaus are required to do for consumers?

Yes. Recent laws have obliged credit bureaus to establish toll-free numbers so that if you have a question or a problem, you can contact them without any charge to you. The law also specifies that the credit bureaus provide a human service representative rather than a computer voice on the other end of the line.

Something else I like, and am sure you will too, is that credit bureaus have to make credit reports easy to understand and readily available. As a consumer you are entitled to all the information in your file with the exception of credit scores, which are usually confidential.

If I am currently disputing a charge with a credit card company, will this appear in my credit report?

Yes. Your credit report also will list the names of the various people or companies that have requested your file within the last six months (or two years if the information was requested by an employer or a potential employer).

What should I be on the lookout for when I receive my credit report?

When you receive your file, review all the information in it to see if everything is accurate. Make a list of everything that is incorrect, out-of-date, or misleading. In particular, look for mistakes in your name, address, phone number, or Social Security number, and for missing or outdated employment information.

If I use the Consumer Credit Counseling Service, will this show up on my credit report?
Yes, it will be reflected on your credit report.

I am getting help from the Consumer Credit Counseling Service. In the eyes of my creditors, is this considered a good thing or is it a black mark?
According to a representative of the CCCS, your creditors see your getting help as both good and bad. First the bad: The fact that you approached the CCCS obviously means that you were in trouble with repaying debt. The good news is that your willingness to use this organization, as opposed to dodging or ignoring your creditors, is very much in your favor. Once you begin making an honest effort to repay your outstanding debts with the help of CCCS, the credit card companies are looking for a consistent record of payment, for anywhere from 12 to 24 months. After that, your credit report starts to look better and better.

What shouldn't be in my credit report?
Be on the lookout for: bankruptcies that are more than ten years old, any negative information about you that is more than seven years old, credit inquiries older than two years, credit accounts that are not yours, incorrect account histories (especially late payments when you've paid on time), a missing notation when you've disputed a charge on a credit card bill, closed accounts incorrectly listed as open, and any account that is not listed as "closed by consumer," because if your re-

port doesn't note this, the account will appear to have been closed by the creditor in question.

What if I find one of these things listed incorrectly on my credit report?

If you find mistakes on your credit report, fill out the "Request for Reinvestigation" form that accompanies your credit report. If you did not receive this form, write to the credit bureau and ask for one. List on the form each incorrect item and explain exactly what is wrong. Be sure to make a copy of the form before sending it back. The reinvestigation is free.

How long will it take the credit bureau to reinvestigate my report?

Once the credit bureau receives your reinvestigation request, it must get back to you within a reasonable time. By law, that usually means 30 days, although many bureaus will get back to you within 10 days. Reinvestigation is an easy process for them, since the bureaus are all linked by computers. If you have found errors—and don't be surprised if you do—you might be concerned that other credit bureaus might also have this misinformation on your credit report. You should play it safe and obtain copies of their reports as well, to make sure any errors are corrected. (See the Additional Resources section at the back of this book for the addresses, phone numbers, and websites of the big three credit bureaus.)

What happens if I don't hear back from the credit bureau?

If you don't hear from the credit bureau within 30 days, send a follow-up letter. Sending a copy of your second letter to the Federal Trade Commission will really grab their attention (see Additional Resources for the FTC's address).

Does the credit bureau have to remove inaccurate information from my credit report?

Yes. If something in your credit report is incorrect, or if the creditor who provided the information can no longer verify it, the credit bureau must remove the information from your file. Often credit bureaus remove information without reinvestigating it if reinvestigation is more bother than it's worth.

Can I add things that I feel are worth mentioning about my financial life to my file?

Absolutely. If you feel the need to explain a particular entry, you are entitled to add a 100-word statement to your file. Because the credit bureau is required to set down only a summary of what you wrote, be extremely concise and clear. You can also add positive things to your file—for example, accounts that you've paid on time. Just ask in writing that the information be added to your report.

My credit bureau seems to be stonewalling me. Do I have any recourse?

If you feel your credit bureau is not abiding by the law or has treated you unfairly, you can send a complaint to the Federal Trade Commission (see Additional Resources for the FTC's address). Be sure to send along a copy of your correspondence with the bureau about which you are complaining. If a credit bureau insists on reporting out-of-date or inaccurate information, writing to the FTC can put an end to it.

I got an offer in the mail for a service that will send me a copy of my credit report anytime I ask for it, for a price. Should I do it?

A lot of firms now offer this kind of credit-monitoring service. They will send you copies of your credit report and a newsletter, and you will also receive various membership services. But I have to ask why a consumer would need this kind of service. Some people, for example those in the middle of a divorce, might want to watch their credit report closely to find out if there are any sudden new flags on it, but most of us don't really need this kind of service. If you want a copy of your credit report, order it from one of the big three credit bureaus.

I just moved from the East Coast to the West Coast. Does this mean a new credit bureau is now handling my credit report? Do I have to tell the credit bureau I've moved?
Since Experian, Trans Union, and Equifax all operate nationally, it probably doesn't make much of a difference where you live. All three agencies have a number of affiliates across the country who end up reporting to them, so most of your information is probably in the files of all three bureaus. As for notifying the credit bureau of your new address, it's not necessary. No doubt you have given this information to the credit card companies. Even if you have not done this yet, many credit bureaus subscribe to the U.S. Post Office's change-of-address service.

Denied Credit

I have good credit, but in search of a better interest rate, I applied for five low-interest-rate credit cards. I was turned down by all of them. How is this possible?
None of these companies were willing to give you a card because this flurry of activity on your part automatically shows up on your credit report and makes lenders very wary. Why?

Because they assumed you were about to go on a major spending spree and put yourself into big-time debt. So they all turned you down. Did it ever occur to them that you might be comparison shopping for credit cards? Of course not. My advice to you now is to wait at least six months before applying for a new credit card but take advantage of being turned down and request a new, free credit report. During this waiting period, check the rates on several different cards and then select one—and only one—card.

I was just denied a credit card and one of the reasons the company gave was "age." I am 35 years old. Is this legal? What's going on here?
A credit card company can take age into consideration when it assesses the application of someone between the ages of 18 and 61. Instead of looking at your application in an individual way, they compare your financial data with that of other people your age. If your "profile" comes up short, you will pay the price.

My aunt, who is 75, recently applied for her first credit card and had a lot of trouble getting one. I would think that elderly people would be the best credit risks of all!
Not as far as the credit card companies are concerned. They are required, however, not to discriminate against older people solely on the basis of age, so if your aunt has a good financial history, she should get the credit she needs. In 1988 in a landmark case, the Federal Trade Commission charged in court that a certain finance company was going against credit protection laws by extending loans to older applicants on far less favorable terms than it offered to younger applicants. Ever since the 1975 passage of the Equal Credit Opportunity Act (ECOA), it has been against the law for a creditor to turn

down an applicant just because he or she is 62 years old or older. The ECOA also requires creditors to figure in income from other sources, such as pensions and annuities, when estimating the financial resources of older citizens—very important factors, since many older people are retired and no longer earning any income from work. It also prevents creditors from changing the terms of a loan or adding interest simply because a person is approaching retirement age. Your aunt should register a complaint against the companies that gave her a hard time with the FTC.

BAD CREDIT RATINGS

I'm slowly realizing that I have a problem with my credit rating. What can I do about it?
If you have a problem with your credit rating, you are not alone. Millions of Americans have been in your position, and millions of Americans have managed to get themselves out of your position. A "bad" credit rating doesn't mean you're a deadbeat or a slacker. You may have run into financial difficulty, or lost your job, two situations that can set a person back temporarily. Or a complicated divorce, a life-threatening illness, or the added expenses of a new child in your family might have affected your credit.

Here are some tips to begin to generate a good credit history for yourself:

- Apply for credit with a local retailer such as a department store.
- Make a large down payment on a purchase and negotiate credit payments for the balance.

- Apply for a small loan at a bank or credit union where you have checking and savings accounts.

If you are rejected for credit, find out why. You may be denied credit for various reasons, including not meeting the creditor's minimum income requirement or not being at your address or job for the required amount of time. You can overcome these obstacles with time.

If you are still unable to get credit, you may wish to ask a friend or relative with an established credit history to act as a cosigner for you. A cosigner promises to repay the debt if you don't. An account established with a cosigner will usually be reported on both of your credit reports.

One thing I would ask you to beware of are so-called "repair clinics." Many states have laws regulating companies that claim they can "repair" your negative credit information. No one can have accurate information removed. You may want to check with your state attorney general or local consumer protection agency before contracting or paying for credit repair services.

Once you have obtained credit, pay your bills consistently and on time. By doing so, you establish a positive credit history that helps you obtain future credit for larger purchases, such as a house or car.

How does a bad credit rating affect a person's day-to-day life?

A bad credit rating can make getting a credit card difficult, and if you can't get a credit card, there are a lot of other things you can't get either. You will run into trouble renting a car, making an airplane reservation, even renting a video. If you don't have a credit card, you may be asked to lay down a sizable amount of money as a deposit, whether it's for that book the store had to special-order, or for such essentials as heat and electricity.

How does a bad credit rating come about in the first place?

A lot of factors, or maybe just one, could have contributed to the situation you find yourself in. It could have been a history of late payments. Or a credit card company may have forgiven that large amount that you were 20 days late in paying, but got pretty annoyed when your balance of $13 took you nearly four months to pay back. Or maybe you didn't pay your balance. There might be notations in your credit rating that you did not honor certain debts that you owed to the IRS, or that you have not paid out a lawsuit that was filed against you that you lost, or that you've fallen behind on child-support payments. Or your bad credit rating could have been caused by something much larger and more serious, like a bankruptcy, which is considered the worst indicator of all on a credit report.

Is there a general definition of "bad" in a credit report, or does every bank look at your credit report and see something different?

You've raised a good point. It's important to remember that every single lender in this country has different standards for lending money to people. These standards are usually confidential, so you never really know what they are, and the banks and the credit unions are the last to tell you. When you think of it this way, there is no such thing, really, as a universally "bad" credit rating. There will be places that you will be denied credit, but there may also be some institutions that are willing to extend you credit.

How do I know if I have a so-so or a bad credit report? What are the warning signs?

Most people who have bad credit reports are usually well aware of the fact—that is, if they are being honest with themselves.

They start to notice a pattern in their financial lives. Credit card companies turn them down left and right. They have a not-very-proud history of getting notices from collection services. The credit card companies that they use have begun calling to find out what happened to that payment that was due three months ago. But there's only one real way to find out if you have a bad credit report—and that is by requesting a copy from one of the big three credit bureaus.

How long will negative information stay on my credit report?

Negative information usually remains on your credit report for seven years. This includes late payments, paid and unpaid lawsuits and judgments, paid and unpaid tax liens, collection or profit-and-loss accounts (an account that a lender has written off as not worth pursuing, but that nevertheless goes on your credit report), and records of arrest, indictment, or conviction of a crime. If you declared Chapter 7 bankruptcy, this information will appear on your credit reports for 10 years—but no longer. All three of the major credit bureaus, however, will remove successfully completed Chapter 13 bankruptcies (this is the case where you have paid back a portion of your debts) seven years from the filing date.

A friend of mine who once declared bankruptcy recently applied for a high-powered job. When her prospective employer looked at her credit report, they turned her down for the job on the basis of the bankruptcy, even though it's 13 years old. Is this legal?

If you are applying for a job with a salary of $75,000 or more, or applying for an insurance policy worth $150,000 or more, or if you're applying for a loan of more than $150,000, there's a very good chance that neither the seven-year or the ten-year time frame will apply and that whatever negative information you've accumulated on your credit report could stay there forever. This is not a legal issue as much as it a fact of life. Think about it: 1.4 million people claim bankruptcy every year. It's virtually impossible for credit bureaus to keep up with the kind of recordkeeping it would require to watch the clock for each and every case to make sure all the negative information is removed when the time's up. So it's up to you to make sure that your information is up to date and accurately reflects your credit standing.

STUDENT LOANS

With all this talk about the pitfalls of debt, I'm thinking twice about applying for a student loan for college. What do you think of student loans?

If you have no other way of paying for your higher education, I think taking out a student loan is one of the best and most honorable investments in your future that you can make. In my opinion, student loans fall in the category of "good debt." Why? Because you are borrowing money for something that you cannot really put a price on—namely, yourself, and your future.

My family has always been proud of its financial independence. I feel there is something slightly shameful about going into debt.

With the price of colleges and universities rising so rapidly, a college education, as an investment, is probably second only to the cost of your house! I bet your family wouldn't think there was anything shameful about getting a mortgage. Similarly, there should be no shame associated with taking out a student loan to pay the full tuition quoted by a college. Between half and three-quarters of all college students pay less than full tuition! You heard me right. I'm talking about students at small colleges in the Midwest as well as at Ivy League universities. Yes, there are a great many forms to fill out—as when you apply for any kind of loan—but remember, you are using what you borrow to invest in yourself and your future.

Is there just one kind of student loan, or are there many different kinds?

There are several kinds of student loans. Probably the oldest and best-known type of student loan is a Perkins loan. In the case of Perkins loans, the U.S. government lends a certain amount of money to a college, which in turn lends to students who need it. The Perkins loan offers a very low—5 percent—interest rate. Then again, this loan is one of the smallest loans out there: It has a ceiling of $3,000 per year, and no more than $15,000 over the course of your undergraduate study. If you are a graduate or a postgraduate student, you can borrow up to $5,000 per year, with a cap of $30,000.

How long do I have to pay off my Perkins loan?

Nine months after you leave college, you have to begin repaying your Perkins loan. You have up to 10 years after that to pay off the full amount. Colleges often sell these loans, with their outstanding balances, to banks. This doesn't mean much for you, except that you will now be making payments to the bank as opposed to the college.

I need a little more money than a Perkins loan can give me. Do I have any options?

You might consider a Stafford loan. Sometimes a Stafford is known as a Federal Family Education Loan (FFEL), or a Ford loan, or a direct loan—it doesn't really matter what you call it, though for the record, if the loan comes from a bank, it is known as an FFEL, and if it comes from a college it is known as a direct loan, or a Ford loan.

Stafford loans exist to make up the difference between the cost of college tuition (whether the college is a two-year or a four-year one) and the expected family contribution, or EFC, which is what a family is supposed to be able to pay after the college has crunched its financials. Freshmen can borrow up to $2,625 at an interest rate that by law can go no higher than 8.25 percent, and which usually hovers around the 7.5 percent mark. The maximum a dependent student (one who has access to parental support) can borrow is $23,000. You begin repaying the loan six months after you leave college, and you have 10 years to pay back the entire amount, though often there is room for negotiation.

To apply for a Stafford loan, you must fill out a form. If you are applying to a bank for the loan, you are required to submit a letter from your college stating your eligibility.

Finally, you should be aware that there are two forms of Stafford loans: subsidized and unsubsidized.

What is the difference between a subsidized and an unsubsidized Stafford loan?

If you receive a subsidized Stafford loan, you will not have to make any interest payments until you begin to repay the loan (six months after you leave college). Until then, the government assumes responsibility for your interest payments. With an unsubsidized Stafford, you (not the government) are responsible for the interest payments while you are at college and for the first six months after you leave. This doesn't mean that you have to pay interest every month; you can defer the interest payments and add them to the principal to be repaid after you have graduated.

My folks have talked to me about taking out a PLUS loan. What is this?

PLUS stands for Parents' Loans for Undergraduate Students. It is a loan with a fairly low interest rate (by law no greater than 9 percent) that your parents can take out that will cover the difference between the cost of attendance (COA), and the amount of financial aid that you will be receiving. The cost of attendance is the total amount it will cost a student to go to school. For full-time students this includes tuition, fees, room and board, allowances for books, supplies, transportation, costs related to dependent care or disability, and miscellaneous expenses. The yearly limit on a PLUS loan is equal to the cost of attendance minus any other financial aid you receive. For example, if your COA is $6,000 and you receive $4,000 in financial aid, your parents could borrow up to but no more than $2,000.

I want to apply for a student loan, but my credit rating isn't that great. Will I run into problems?

Oddly enough, you probably won't. If you—or your family— has had a checkered history of bill-paying, it will not count against you. The same goes for bankruptcy. The only thing that could count against you is if you ever defaulted on a previous student loan. Your only qualifications for a Stafford or a Perkins loan are:

- need
- a high school diploma or GED

- enrollment or acceptance for enrollment as a regular student working toward a degree or certificate in an eligible program
- U.S. citizenship or eligible noncitizen status
- a valid Social Security number

Please note: If you are a veteran, or the child of a veteran who died or was permanently disabled in battle, or a nursing student, a pharmacy student, or a Native American, special grants and dispensations are available to you. Check with your college or university.

Who exactly grants and manages my loan—the department of education or a bank?

Who your loan holder will be depends on the type of loan you take out. If you take out a Perkins loan, your loan will be managed by the school that lends you the money or by an agency that the school assigns to service the loan. If you take out a direct loan, the funds for your loan are lent to you directly by the U.S. government and it will be managed by the Direct Loan Servicing Center. If you borrow a FFEL Program Loan, the funds for your loan are lent to you from a bank, credit union, or other lender that participates in the FFEL Program, and it will be managed by your lender or its servicing agent. Your lender or the Direct Loan Servicing Center will provide you with additional information about your loan.

POSTPONING OR CANCELING STUDENT LOAN PAYMENTS

If I really cannot make my payments, is there anything I can do?

Yes. A variety of options may be available to you. These options range from having your loan canceled, which means you do not have to ever pay it back (this is almost impossible), to getting what is known as a deferment, or a forbearance. What you can or cannot do depends on what kind of loan you have as well as the reason you cannot pay.

Under what circumstance can a student loan be canceled?

A student loan can be canceled if you are permanently disabled or die.

What is a deferment?

A deferment of a student loan simply means that you defer the loan payment, or wait until a later date to make it. During that time, no interest accrues (in most cases).

Under what conditions may a loan be deferred and/or canceled?

These conditions will vary with each loan and when you obtained it, but in general your loan could be deferred if you, your spouse, or one of your dependents became disabled; if you went back to school part-time; if, for whatever reason, you were currently unemployed; or if you have young children. If you are suffering an economic hardship, you can probably get a deferment of up to three years if you have a federal loan. If you join the U.S. military you could qualify for a deferment or even, under certain circumstances, a cancellation. You also might qualify to have your loan deferred or canceled if you get a job in law enforcement, or if you become a teacher dealing with the underprivileged or needy, or if you get a job in the health-care profession and in a part of the country where there is a shortage of health-care workers. You also can get a deferment or a cancellation if you decide to perform community service, such as serving in the Peace Corps. Finally, you could get a deferment if you enrolled in a rehabilitation program for the disabled, and you are automatically eligible if you are on SSI or are getting any kind of public assistance. Again, please note that each situation is different, based on the kind of loan you have as well as when you obtained the loan. Call the holder of your loan and ask under what circumstances you would qualify for a deferment of your loan.

If I have been in default on my loan, can I still apply for a deferment?

No. If you have been late in making your payments a few times and you are not in default, you may be eligible for what is called a retroactive deferment. If you are in default, you will not be able to get a deferment.

How do I cancel my loan?

If you have called the loan holder and you feel you qualify for a cancellation, you must apply for it. Call the Department of Education's Debt Collection Services Office at (800) 621-3115 and request an application. Fill it out and return it with all the paperwork they will request.

How do I defer my loan?

You also have to apply for a deferment. Call the holder of your loan and tell them why you think you qualify for a deferment. They will then send you the appropriate paperwork.

If I apply for a deferment, forbearance, or a cancellation of my loan, can I stop making payments at that time?

No matter whether you are applying for a deferment, cancellation, or forbearance, you must continue to make payments until you are notified that the request has been granted. If you don't, you may end up in default. You should keep a copy of any request form you submit, and you should document all contacts with the organization that holds or manages your loan.

If I get a deferment, how long will I be allowed to defer my payments?

Usually about six months to one year. The economic hardship deferral is for three years but, as always, each case will be different depending on the kind of deferment, and what kind of loan you have and when you got it.

If I get a deferment and I need to apply for another one, can I?

Yes. Each time you are granted a deferment, the holder of the loan will let you know how long that deferral will be and when you should re-apply, if necessary.

In a deferment, does the interest on my loan keep accumulating?

In most cases, no.

If I do not qualify for a deferment or a cancellation, is there anything else I can do?

Yes. You can apply for what is known as a forbearance. A forbearance is very much like a deferment in that you are allowed to put off making payments for a certain length of time. But with a forbearance interest *always* continues to accrue during the time you are not making payments. Also, with a forbearance it does not matter when you obtained the loan or what kind of loan it is, which makes a forbearance far easier to get than a deferment.

I have been in default and I know I cannot get a deferral. Can I get a forbearance?

Yes. You can get a forbearance even if you have been in default.

If I have a number of loans, do I have to get a forbearance on each of them?

No. The number of loans that you will apply for a forbearance on will depend on how much money you are short. Since the interest continues to accumulate while you are not making payments on those loans, you have to be very careful. If you have many loans, apply for a forbearance on the lowest-interest-rate loans first. It may seem better to postpone the higher-interest-rate loans, but it is not in the long run. Remember, the interest is still ticking away, adding up. Again, get a forbearance on the lowest-interest-rate loans first.

My loan payments are currently more than 20 percent of my gross income. Can I get a forbearance?

Yes. When your loan payments are 20 percent or more of your gross income, your loan holder is actually required to give you a forbearance if you want one.

How long can I have a forbearance?

The length of time you can have a forbearance varies according to the loan holder, but the time period is usually up to three years.

DEFAULTING ON A STUDENT LOAN

More than 20 years ago, I took out student loans. I've never paid them back and I've never heard from anyone. Will the same be true for my children if they do not pay back their student loans?

I'm afraid not. It used to be true that if you took out a student loan and did not pay it back, chances were very good that you wouldn't ever hear from anyone. But that is no longer true. If your children do not pay back the money they borrowed, they will hear about it immediately and will suffer financial consequences in a big way.

If you default on your loan, your school, the lender or agency that holds your loan, the state, and the federal government may all take action to recover the money, including notifying national credit bureaus of your default. This may affect your credit rating for a long time. For example, you may find it very difficult to borrow from a bank to buy a car or a house. In addition, the lender or agency holding your loan may ask your employer to deduct payments from your paycheck. Also, you may be liable for expenses incurred in collecting the loan. If you decide to return to school, you're not entitled to receive any more federal student aid. The U.S. Department of Education may ask the U.S. Internal Revenue Service to withhold your income tax refund, and the amount of your refund will be applied toward the amount you owe.

When exactly am I considered to be in default?

You are not usually considered to be in default until you have not made your student loan payments or had any contact with the loan holder to apply for a deferment, forbearance, or cancellation for at least six months.

If I have not repaid my student loans for years and the interest and penalties have mounted up, can I negotiate to get those penalties dropped or reduced?

You can try, but chances are you will not get anywhere. To my knowledge, student loan holders seldom negotiate or make a deal. They do not have to, nor, truthfully, should they. If you take out a loan, you should adhere to the terms of that loan.

I am about to default on my student loans. What will happen to me if I do?

If you do default on your student loans, you could be sued by your loan holder. If you are working, or ever do work, up to 10 percent of your wages will be garnished, and if you are due a tax refund it will be taken to pay your student loans. Furthermore, your credit rating will be affected, and that could affect your getting a mortgage, or rental apartment, among other things.

Is there a way for me to get out of default?

Yes: by making 12 consecutive monthly payments on your loan. Not only will you then be able to apply for a deferment, but you can also request that your default be cleared from your credit report.

I am in default. I want to pay off my student loan, but I just cannot afford the current monthly amount that is due. Will my lender adjust the amount for me?

By law, you are not required to pay back more on your student loans than you can reasonably afford. Gather all your financial paperwork and call your lender and ask about what is called a reasonable and affordable repayment plan. Depending on your financial situation, your lender could allow you to pay as little as $5 a month.

What happens if I am granted this reasonable and affordable plan?

If you keep on schedule and make at least six monthly payments in a row, you will be eligible for new federal student loans. After 12 monthly payments, you will not be in default anymore. Then you are eligible to apply for a deferral.

I am currently in default on two of my student loans but not on a third. Can I consolidate my loans?

Yes, you can. In fact, if you were to refinance or consolidate your loans, you would no longer be in default on those two loans.

WAGE GARNISHMENT

If I default on a student loan and I am working, does the Department of Education have legal authority to garnish my wages?

Yes. And not only the Department of Education but also the agencies that guarantee your loans have the right to take up to a total of 10 percent of your wages.

I thought I had to be sued and get a court judgment in order for my wages to be garnished.

That is true of all loans except student loans. If you default on any other kind of loan, your creditor(s) can garnish your wages up to 25 percent if they get a court judgment against you. Remember, even if the Department of Education does sue you and gets that court judgment they are not allowed to take more than 10 percent of your wages.

Will I know in advance if my wages are going to be garnished, or will it just happen one day?

You will be notified beforehand. The Department of Education is obliged to let you know in writing 30 days before the garnishment date. They must inform you how much you owe them, how you may enter into a repayment schedule so your wages are not garnished, and how you can obtain a hearing on this garnishment process to try to stop it.

How long do I have to respond to their letter?

You have approximately 15 days to respond to the Department of Education, and your response must be in writing.

If the Department of Education is going to garnish my wages, at what point will they let my employer know?

The Department of Education will let your employer know they are going to garnish your wages about 20 business days after you receive their notice. They assume you will receive their notice by five business days from the date they mailed it.

If I have just started a new job after not working for the past year, can my wages be garnished?

Yes. But if you were fired or laid off and did not return to work for an entire full year, you can object to this garnishment and you may win.

I barely make enough to live on now. How can my wages be garnished?

If you do not earn at least 30 times the federal minimum wage per week, your wages cannot be garnished.

How many days can I be in default before my wages can be garnished?

You can be in default about 225 days before your wages will be garnished.

I have been in default for some time, and I seem to have slipped through the cracks. When is the statute of limitations up?

Never. If you haven't paid your student loan, you are still responsible for it, and any interest on it, too.

If I have been in default all these years, why hasn't the Department of Education come after me?

The Department of Education usually doesn't pursue people in default if it would cost them more than they would collect or if those in default do not have the money (or other assets).

If the Department of Education sues me and I lose, what can they get?

Almost everything: your bank account, your car, as well as any other property and/or assets—and, again, they can garnish your wages.

If I am being harrassed by a collection agency because I'm in default on a student loan, what should I do?

Call the Deputy Director of Debt Collections at (202) 708-4766. If the harrassment continues, contact the Policy Development Division, Loan Branch of the U.S. Department of Education at (202) 708-8242.

STUDENT LOANS AND BANKRUPTCY

I have been told that if I claim bankruptcy I will not be able to get rid of my student loan. Is that true?

That is now true. A few years ago, your student loan might have been excused if you declared bankruptcy, depending when that loan first came due. Now, no student loans, regardless of when they came due, can be dismissed because of bankruptcy. The *only* exception to this rule is if paying back the student loan will cause you what is considered undue hardship. But bankruptcy courts have very strict definitions of undue hardship, and in many cases, if you meet those definitions, you probably would qualify to have your loan canceled. Bottom line: You probably would be better off trying to get your student loan canceled than filing for bankruptcy just to get your student loan discharged.

What kinds of loans cannot be discharged in bankruptcy court?

Any loan that was issued and funded/guaranteed and/or insured by a government entity or nonprofit corporation—such as student loans, FHA loans, and IRS debts—cannot be dismissed by a bankruptcy court.

If I claim Chapter 13, can I include my student loan payments in my repayment plan?

Yes, but be careful. Chapter 13 bankruptcy allows an individual who has consumer (household) debts to make a plan to pay creditors, but there are limits to the amount of debt and other restrictions with this form of bankruptcy filing. Remember, your student loan cannot be discharged in the same way as some of your other loans. Under Chapter 13, some of your creditors will not get back the full amount that you owe them by the end of the payment period, but in essence your loan will be discharged. This is not true of student loans. If you choose to pay back only a small amount per month, at the end of Chapter 13 bankruptcy, you will still owe the balance on your student loans.

TAKING CONTROL
OF YOUR DEBT

If I realize that my debt is starting to spiral out of control, should I cut up my credit cards?
Absolutely. Take out a pair of scissors and cut up each and every credit card in your wallet right now. Are you hesitating? If you feel that you simply can't survive without your credit cards, you might think seriously about calling Debtors Anonymous (you can find their telephone number as well as their address and website in the Additional Resources section).

What is Debtors Anonymous?
Debtors Anonymous, or DA, is an excellent nationwide organization that models itself on the 12-step program of Alcoholics Anonymous. You attend DA meetings with people who are in the same boat as you and who are making an honest, concerted effort to get rid of debt in their lives. For many people, DA meetings are the first time they realize they are not alone in debt. DA can be very helpful, particularly if used in

conjunction with the Consumer Credit Counseling Service, or CCCS (see the Additional Resources section for their address, phone number, and website).

What exactly does the Consumer Credit Counseling Service do?

The CCCS is an accredited nonprofit agency that assists consumers who are in trouble with debt. Like DA, they are nationwide. For a modest fee, from $5 to $35—though the fee may be waived if you cannot pay it—a CCCS counselor will sit down with you and discuss all the elements of your debt, review all your options, and help you figure out the best way to get out of debt. Sometimes they will even negotiate with creditors on your behalf, establish a debt management plan, and advise you of the possible consequences of declaring bankruptcy.

What is a debt management plan?

A debt management plan, or DMP, is a voluntary arrangement between you, your creditors, and the Consumer Credit Counseling Service. A DMP does two things at once: It helps you get out of debt in an honorable, organized way, and it helps your creditors get back the money you owe them. Here's how it works: A consumer agrees to deposit a certain amount of money each month in an account that the CCCS oversees, and the CCCS distributes this money among the consumer's creditors. Incidentally, if you enter into a DMP, many creditors will agree to lower their interest rates and fees, and in some cases eliminate them altogether. Your CCCS counselor can fill you in on the details of your credit card companies' policies.

Can any other agencies help me out?

Yes. You also can get in touch with the Debt Counselors of America, or DCA (see the Additional Resources section at the back of this book). DCA has both counselors and lawyers on staff. The latter can give you general consumer information, though because of state laws, they are not permitted to give you legal advice.

I'm scared not to have at least one credit card to carry around with me. What if I get into some kind of an emergency situation?

If you feel this way, cut up all but one of your credit cards and carry this card in case of emergencies. You can safeguard against overspending with this card by calling the credit card company and asking them to lower your credit limit. Pick an amount of credit you would like to have in case of an emergency (say, $500 or $1,000), and ask the company to set your limit. Alternatively, carry an American Express card that must be paid off in full every month. You wouldn't stock your kitchen with cookies and cakes if you were dieting, would you? So why keep credit cards you don't need and don't want to be tempted to use?

Okay, I've cut up all my credit cards and put the pieces in the garbage. Now what?

Good! Now sit down with your debt, study your statements, face what you owe, and see what the credit card companies are charging you to owe it. Make a list of all the amounts of money you owe in descending order, starting with the amounts with the highest interest charges. Include all your creditors—and I mean *everybody,* from Visa to your sister. Don't forget to include personal debt on your list, because remember: Debt is debt, and just because most personal debt doesn't inspire the fear or paranoia of credit card debt, on the self-respect scale it weighs in pound for pound. List the amount you owe, the interest rate, the minimum monthly payment, and how your creditor charges you interest (average daily or two-cycle average daily). Also list the phone numbers of all your creditors. For example:

CREDITOR	BALANCE OWED	INTEREST RATE	PAYMENT	CYCLE	PHONE
Dept. store	$4,320	21%	$180	Avg. daily	
Visa	$6,300	18.9%	$200	2-cycle	
Dept. store	$3,100	16.9%	$100	2-cycle	
Optima	$4,000	7.9%	$120	Avg. daily	
Mom	$5,000	0	0	0	

I've listed all my debts and I realize I owe late payments to some of my creditors. What should I do?

This is where the phone numbers come in. If you're late making a payment on any of your debts, personal or institutional, call up the person or institution you've borrowed money from right now. Tell them why your payment is late. Your creditors already know you don't have the money to pay the bill or else you would have, so don't be embarrassed. You're not a failure or a bad person, you are simply someone who hasn't handled his or her money well. If the person on the other end of the line is rude to you, be gracious and explain your situation. Perhaps your payment is late but you will have the money in two weeks. Or maybe you can send only $25. In any case, it's important that you call your creditors before they call you.

What if I'm not late with my payments? Should I call the credit card companies anyway?

If you want to try to lower your interest rates, it's worth a try. Call the high-interest-rate credit card companies, tell them you're considering switching to a better value card, and see if they'll match a lower rate. You can negotiate with them, and often they will reduce your interest rate right on the spot. If they won't, simply move your balance to a card that does offer a lower interest rate. Make sure you cancel the first card after you've transferred your balance.

I'm looking at the list of what I owe, and it makes me sick. I don't think I'll ever get out of this mess.

Don't panic. You can get out of it and you will, too, a step—or a month—at a time. The best way to start—one that most people are not aware of—is to pay more than the minimum balance due each month.

Why is paying more than the minimum monthly balance so important?

The numbers say it all. Let's say you owe $1,100 on a card that charges you 18.5 percent interest. If you pay the minimum 1.7 percent every month and you never charge another thing, it will take you twelve years and six months to pay off your debt. That's a very long time! And your $1,100 balance will have cost you about $1,400 in interest. If, however, you had paid $10 more than the minimum each month, you would have reduced your payment period to six years and cut your total interest payments to $676.37. Ten dollars a month is only 35 cents a day, but it adds up to a savings in interest of about $800.

I'm always shopping around for a lower interest rate, but are you saying that an even better tactic is to pay the credit card companies more than the minimum payment each month?

No, both are extremely important. With most credit cards, the more you owe, and the higher the interest rate, the longer it takes you to pay everything off. This is compounded interest working against you. In some cases, if you owed $4,000 or more and you had an 18 percent interest rate, and you paid just the minimum every month, it would take you 40 years to pay off the debt, to say nothing of the thousands and thousands in interest it would cost you—to say nothing of the 40-year weight on your shoulders!

Below is a chart that will show you, pretty conclusively, what a difference a little more money each month can really make.

ANNUAL PERCENTAGE RATE	MONTHLY PAYMENT	AMOUNT OF TIME REQUIRED TO PAY OFF DEBT	TOTAL INTEREST PAID
5.9	$100	45 months	$465
5.9	$110	40 months	$417
5.9	$150	29 months	$298
5.9	$200	22 months	$221
7.9	$100	47 months	$658
7.9	$110	42 months	$587
7.9	$150	30 months	$413
7.9	$200	22 months	$303
9.9	$100	49 months	$874
9.9	$110	44 months	$775
9.9	$150	31 months	$536
9.9	$200	21 months	$389
12.9	$100	53 months	$1,257
12.9	$110	47 months	$1,101
12.9	$150	32 months	$739
12.9	$200	23 months	$528
15.9	$100	58 months	$1,736
15.9	$110	50 months	$1,494

Annual Percentage Rate	Monthly Payment	Amount of Time Required to Pay Off Debt	Total Interest Paid
15.9	$150	34 months	$968
15.9	$200	24 months	$678
18.9	$100	63 months	$2,362
18.9	$110	54 months	$1,986
18.9	$150	35 months	$1,229
18.9	$200	25 months	$842

BORROWING TO REPAY DEBT

401(K), OR RETIREMENT PLAN

Can I borrow from my 401(k) to pay off my credit card debts?

Many employers will allow you to borrow up to 50 percent of the money in your 401(k), or retirement, plan, up to $50,000, to pay for a house or a college education, for other situations that qualify. This loan, you should know, does not come interest-free; interest rates are generally reasonable and set by your company. Ask your human resources department if you can borrow from your 401(k) to pay off your credit card debt.

What are the advantages of borrowing from my 401(k)?

One of the biggest advantages of borrowing money from your 401(k), for whatever purpose, is that since you are effectively borrowing your *own* money, from yourself, the interest you pay, as well as the principal, goes right back to you. Also, when you borrow from your 401(k), you have five years to pay back the money (rather than the 40 years it could take you by paying the minimum on some credit cards). Usually you will pay yourself about 2 percent above the prime rate, the basic interest rate set by the government.

If I borrow money from my 401(k), won't this prevent my 401(k) from increasing in value?

Yes, you could be losing out on the growth potential of your money depending on what the markets are doing. If you are paying 18.5 or 21 percent on your credit cards, and you can't transfer your balance to a lower-interest-rate card because of a bad credit report, you might actually lose less money by borrowing from yourself at 8 or 9 percent, missing out on some growth for a while, and starting over again clean.

Are there other disadvantages of borrowing money from my 401(k)?

One possible downside is that if you happen to leave your job or get fired, the money you borrowed is due in one lump sum within 30 to 90 days of your departure. If you do not have the money to pay it back at that time, your remaining loan amount will be taxable to you as ordinary income. Also, if you are younger than 59½, you will pay a 10 percent penalty tax.

HOME EQUITY LOAN

What about taking out a home equity loan to pay off my credit card debt?

A home equity loan is another option, with its own advantages. A home equity loan could be at a lower interest rate than your credit card, and often that interest is tax-deductible, so you'll have converted a high-interest, non–tax-deductible debt to a lower-interest, tax-deductible debt. The problem with this, however, if you do not have your credit card spending under control, before you know it, you will have charged your cards to the max again, *and* have a home equity loan to pay. You have effectively doubled your debt load.

If I have $50,000 equity in my home, can I take out a $50,000 home equity loan?

No. You can't automatically get a home equity loan equal to the amount of equity you have in your home. Most banks will allow you to borrow only 80 percent of the value of your house, less all current mortgage balances. If your house is worth $200,000, 80 percent of its value is $160,000. Subtract the $150,000 you owe on your mortgage, and this gives you the amount you can get as a home equity loan (if you qualify): in this case, $10,000. You qualify for a home equity loan depending on the amount of equity you have in your home as well as your ability to meet your other debts and financial obligations.

I have a friend whose bank let him borrow more than 80 percent of the value of his home.

Some banks want you to borrow 80 percent or more of the value of your home, and it can turn out to be quite costly for you. Most mortgage companies that lend more than 80 percent will make you pay what is called private mortgage insurance, or PMI, which will add quite a bit to the loan—so it's best if you can stick to the straight 80 percent loans, which after all are based on what lenders think you can comfortably afford. If you want to get around PMI, find a good mortgage broker.

EQUITY LINE OF CREDIT

How about an equity line of credit?

An equity line of credit will enable you to borrow money as you need it against the value of your house.

How is an equity line of credit different from a home equity loan?

A home equity loan has a fixed interest rate while an equity line of credit usually has a rate that varies according to what interest rates are doing. The payback period for an equity line of credit is not set—so make sure you're extremely disciplined if you consider this alternative. With this type of loan, you do not have to pay back principal each month if you don't want to; you can pay just the interest. A home equity loan, on the other hand, works pretty much like a regular mortgage. You get a fixed interest rate and pay back the loan over a set period of time, usually five to fifteen years.

A COMPARISON

How should I decide whether to borrow from my 401(k) or take out a home equity loan?

Before doing either, ask yourself how disciplined you are. After all, it may have been lack of discipline that got you into debt in the first place. With a 401(k) loan you don't really have much of a choice: You have to pay back the loan in five years. Home equity loans, on the other hand, can go on for up to fifteen years. It's up to you to make sure you don't let the loan drag on for fifteen years, that you stick to a maximum payback period of five years, just as you would with a 401(k) loan. If you promise yourself you will do this, and if the interest rate is favorable compared with your credit card's interest rate, a home equity loan may be better than borrowing from your 401(k).

What are the tax consequences of borrowing from my 401(k)? And are there any other consequences I should keep in mind?

If you borrow money from your 401(k) to pay off your credit card debt, you will be taxed twice on the loan amount. The money you borrow is money you contributed to your retirement plan before taxes, but you pay the loan off with after-tax money (unlike your contributions, your loan payments are not deducted from your paycheck before taxes). When you withdraw your 401(k) money for retirement, it will be taxed again. If at all possible, if you borrow from your 401(k), please try your best to make your normal contributions as well as your loan payments, or your long-term loss may be too great.

Let's look at what a loan can do to your retirement savings. Say you are 35 years old, you make $40,000 a year, and you have a 401(k) balance of $20,000. You contribute $2,400, or 6 percent of your salary, per year, and your employer match is $1,400. Assume that you get an annual return of 8 percent on your account. If you continue saving at this rate until age 65, your retirement nest egg will be about $583,723.

But you have your eye on a new car! You could afford a compact car, but you really crave one of those new SUVs with a CD player. So you take out a $10,000 loan on your 401(k), with the intention of paying it back over five years. But you can't afford to continue making your contributions while you are paying back your loan. So, when you reach age 65, guess how much your account will be worth? $458,673. That difference of roughly $127,000 in principal translates into a loss of $7,620 a year in retirement income, assuming returns of 6 percent. That's about $630 a month, which is quite a chunk of cash. Are you convinced?

Yes. But I will be continuing to make contributions to my retirement account, as well as paying back the loan.

Could you break down the preliminary charges for the 401(k) loan versus the home equity loan?

Gladly. With a 401(k) loan, fees are variable: Some employers will charge you for taking out the loan and some won't. Some make you pay a fee of up to $100 just to fill out the paperwork, and some charge a yearly fee while the loan is outstanding. The same is true of home equity loans: Some can be gotten for no fees except for an appraisal on your home (at a cost of $200 to $300), and some will charge you fees up front to take out the loan or for the paperwork, which can add another $100 or $200 to the bill. But if you look carefully, you should be able to find a home equity loan that can be had for no fees, no points, and a very small appraisal fee, if any.

Is there any difference in the application process?

Applying for either kind of loan is usually fairly easy. You may have to fill out a form, or you may be able to apply over the phone. However, loans from either source take time to process, so if you're desperate, ask your employer and your lender respectively how long a 401(k) loan and a home equity loan will take to process and when you will have the money in hand.

If I take out a 401(k) loan, who decides which of my investments are sold off?

Who decides which of your investments are cashed in depends on your company's internal policies. Some companies will let you decide; others will make a decision for you. If you have any doubts about how this works in your company, ask your benefits adviser in your human resources department. If you do have a choice of which investments to liquidate, I would start liquidating the money that is parked in either money market funds or bond funds and then move on to your worst-performing growth funds, essentially moving up the return scale of your 401(k) plan. If, after the bond funds have been cashed in, you're unsure of how your other funds have been performing, or if all your money is in growth funds or company stock, request a summary of the latest investment returns of the investments in the 401(k) plan from your human resources department. Check the funds that you have your money invested in and compare their overall returns for one year, three years, five years, and, if available, ten years. See which funds overall have had the highest and most consistent returns, and which have had the lowest returns. Start liquidating the ones that have the lowest returns and move up from there until you have liquidated the money you need.

Which makes more financial sense: taking out a home equity loan or borrowing from my 401(k)?
This is a bottom-line decision. Take a look at the following chart, and see how the two of them measure up:

	401(K) LOAN	HOME EQUITY LOAN
Tax-deductible	No	Yes
Payback period	5 years	5 to 15 years
Subject to income tax if not paid back	Yes	No
Due/Payable if you leave current employer	Yes	No
Giving up potential growth	Yes	No

Now consider the actual numbers. Let's examine what it means to borrow $10,000 at 9 percent interest (assuming a 28 percent tax bracket). In both scenarios, the payback period is five years.

	401(K) LOAN	HOME EQUITY LOAN
Monthly payment	$ 208	$ 208
Number of payments	60	60
Total paid	$12,455	$12,455
Total interest paid	$ 2,455	$ 2,455
Tax savings (at 28%)	0	$ 687

Because of the tax savings, the home equity loan looks better than borrowing from my 401(k). But what happens if over these five years the amount in my 401(k) goes down rather than up? At what rate of return does it make more sense to borrow from my 401(k)?

Neither you nor I can really predict the movement of the market. All we can do is play it. And the odds still fall pretty much in favor of a home equity loan. An 8 to 10 percent tax-deductible home equity loan usually works out better as long as your money in the 401(k) does not earn more than 6 to 8 percent. The variables here are the size of the loan, how much you would pay in interest on your home equity loan, how much you would pay to borrow from your 401(k), and what tax bracket you are in. Run the numbers for yourself and consult a financial adviser before you choose.

Remember, however, that whether you borrow from your 401(k) or take out a home equity loan, the money isn't a windfall. In either case, you are borrowing from yourself and paying yourself back! Call it what you will: This money is plain old debt, debt to help you get out of even worse debt.

What happens if I cannot pay back the loan to my 401(k)?

Most 401(k) plans have a five-year window for repayment of any loans. If you can't pay back the amount that you borrowed in that time, your loan is considered in default and the outstanding balance is considered by your employer and by the IRS as a taxable withdrawal. In short, you will pay taxes on the money as if it were ordinary income. And if you're under age 59½, you may also have to pay a 10 percent early withdrawal penalty on the amount you haven't paid back. This is a potentially vicious circle, since it often obliges individual consumers to cash in even more of their 401(k) plan assets—which are also taxable, and subject to the same possible early withdrawal penalties.

What happens if I cannot pay back my home equity loan?

It is quite possible that the bank will attach a lien on your house, which means that you will not be able to sell the house until the loan is paid back.

COLLECTION AGENCIES

I am in deep trouble with debt. I can't pay my credit card bills or my car loan. Is somebody going to throw me into jail?

No. A creditor can't put you in jail because you can't pay your bills. But they can do a lot of other things, such as turn your account over to a collection agency, take you to court to sue for the amount that is due them, garnish your wages, or foreclose on your house. Credit card companies can be really tough when it comes to collecting the money they are owed. Outside collection agencies are federally regulated, but there are few laws that govern how a creditor that wants to get its money back can operate.

Are debt collectors thugs who would rather intimidate me than have me pay back the money I owe?

In most cases, debt collectors are professionals performing a necessary service. Still, a debt collection agency can bother and even instill fear in many consumers.

How long do I have before a credit card company will turn my account over to a collection agency?

Usually, if your credit card account is two weeks late, you will receive a friendly reminder in the mail or sometimes even a phone call from the credit card company. If after two months you haven't paid the minimum due on your account, it's very likely you'll get another letter, this time less friendly, and perhaps several more phone calls. At this point, your card might be frozen—which means you can't rack up any more purchases until this matter has been resolved to the credit card company's satisfaction. After three or four months of delinquency, a lot of creditors will consider your account a "bad debt." This means that you haven't responded satisfactorily to their letters and phone calls or that you promised to pay and you didn't, and now the card company is willing to take other steps to get back the money you owe them. This is when the collection companies come in.

What do the collection agencies want from me?

Collection agencies have only one purpose in life: They are in the business of getting you to pay back your debts. Usually they work on commission, receiving a portion of what they manage to collect. Sometimes they will turn their cases over to a lawyer, who will draft a letter warning you that if you do not pay off your delinquent balance at once, you will be taken to court. Once your account has gone to a collection agency, you have lost the opportunity to negotiate with the credit card company. If you call the card company, they will simply refer you to the collection agency.

What if I don't hear from the collection agency for a while? Does this mean I'm off the hook?

If you don't hear from the collection company for a while, don't assume they have forgotten about you and gone on to other, more important things. Some collections begin years after the inception of a debt.

I am being pursued by a collection agency. Are there any laws governing how a collection agency can behave?

Yes. In 1978, Congress passed the Fair Debt Collection Practices Act in order to prevent customers from being shaken down by collection companies. This act also puts reins on some of the tactics they may use. Please note: The Fair Debt Collection Practices Act applies to outside collection agencies, the ones that most credit card companies hire after their own attempts have failed—and not the collection department within the card company.

What are collectors and collection agencies not allowed to do?

Collectors cannot phone your home over and over again. They cannot call you before 8 A.M. or after 9 P.M. They cannot threaten you or use obscene language. Collectors and collection agencies are not allowed to call your friends, your neighbors, and the people you work with to spread rumors about you or tell people about your financial situation.

Please note: If you're being harrassed by a collection agency because you haven't repaid your student loan, see the Additional Resources section for agencies to contact for help.

My collection agency does everything they are not supposed to do. Can I sue them?
Yes, you can sue a collection agency—if you can afford it. Remember, lawsuits can be expensive, so you might want to take them to small claims court instead. Make sure you know the laws and when it makes sense to go to court and when it does not. Remember, the abuse has to occur over a sustained period of time, not just one day. Make sure you have documentation and witnesses. You will need both if you plan to take a collection agency to court.

I got seriously behind in my payments to my credit card companies, and they turned them over to a collection agency. Ever since then, I have been fighting off collectors. I've been making small payments every month in an amount I can afford, but these collectors call me day and night, even at my workplace. I have told them I'm paying my debts to the best of my ability and asked them to stop harassing me, but this seems to do absolutely no good. Do I have any legal rights?
Yes. The Federal Fair Debt Collection Practices Act (FDCPA) will help you if the collector is a collection agency and not the creditor itself. What you should do is write the collection agency the following letter, taken from John Cioffi's *Protecting Your Credit.*

As you know, Section 805a (1) [of the Fair Debt Collection Practices Act] states, "Without the prior consent of a consumer given directly to the debt collector or the express permission of a court of competent jurisdiction, a debt collector may not communicate with a consumer in connection with the collection of any debt at any unusual time or place or at a time or place known or which should be known to be inconvient to the consumer." I am emphatically stating that at my place of work, my home, or anywhere else regarding this matter is inconvenient to me. Your failure to comply with this request will subject your organization to civil liberty under the Fair Debt Collection Practices Act, Section 813, which is $500,000 or 1 percent of your net worth, whichever is less.

All dialogue from this moment on will be conducted through the U.S. Mail only.

I have written a letter like the one above, but I'm still being harassed. What can I do?
Contact the Federal Trade Commission and register a formal complaint. Make sure you document every time they call, for if you can prove their continued harassment, that collection agency is open to a lawsuit—one you could win if you have the proper documentation or proof of the harassment. There have been several successful suits against collectors where the consumer won in court.

Do I have any other legal actions against a collection agency?
If you think that the collection agency is behaving in a way that you suspect is illegal, write a letter to the Federal Trade Commission, including as many details as possible. Send a copy of this letter to the state attorney general's office or to your local consumer-protection office, or both. You might also

consider sending a copy of this letter to the legal department of the credit card company that started this ball rolling in the first place. If this fails, contact the American Collectors Association (see Additional Resources for contact information), whose members agree to conduct their business in a professional manner.

BANKRUPTCY

Who is bankruptcy for, exactly?

Bankruptcy is for all of us, if we find ourselves in a financial situation we can't see our way out of. It's for consumers who can't pay back all their debts. It's for people who can't pay their bills. There are different forms of bankruptcy for different circumstances. Two of the most common are Chapter 7, in which all your debts (except student loans and taxes) are excused, and Chapter 13, in which filing for bankruptcy gives you the opportunity to work out repayment schedules that are fair to you and your creditors, while protecting your assets from being seized by your creditors. Bankruptcy offers you breathing room and another crack at a responsible financial life.

I'm deeply in debt, and I'm thinking of filing for bankruptcy. If I do, will the consequences be significant?

Filing for bankruptcy has sizable and long-term emotional as well as financial consequences. It is not referred to as the "10-year mistake" for nothing! I want to emphasize that bankruptcy is not to be taken lightly. I consider it an option reluctantly, after much thought, and when—and *only* when—there is no other way out.

What kinds of questions should I ask myself before filing for bankruptcy?

Filing for bankruptcy may help you with your money problems, but it doesn't help those to whom you owe money. Imagine how you'd feel if someone who owed you a lot of money sent you a letter saying, "Sorry, I'm bankrupt, I won't be paying you back." Whom do you owe money? Credit card companies? Friends? Businesses? Will you have to see these people after you claim bankruptcy, and if so, how will that make you feel? What financial hardship, if any, will you put others into if you take such an action? Is there absolutely no other way that you can climb out of debt little by little with some work and effort? Are you just looking for a quick fix?

I'm in debt because of overspending on my credit cards. I really don't owe that much, but I'm thinking of filing bankruptcy so I can start over. Is this a good idea?

This is a question that goes deeper than your financial record. If you are thinking about declaring bankruptcy, remember this: If you do not pay your debts, someone else will have to. It might be the bank or the credit card companies who will have to absorb the money you owe them. Your debt might be passed along to the rest of us. It could affect the scoring system that credit bureaus use, which means that someone you don't even know could be turned down for a credit card because of your mistakes. Declaring bankruptcy is not simply a way to erase your spending mistakes and start over. You must understand that fact not just for your own sake but for the sake of the rest of us, who will surely, one way or another, be required to pick up the pieces.

I feel terrible even considering bankruptcy, but years of unplanned medical bills have forced me to this point!

I understand. Terrible things—illness, death, natural disaster, or a financial blow—can strike any of us, unexpectedly. Bankruptcy laws take this into consideration—in fact, they exist to help people in situations like these. If you've faced great adversity, you should be permitted to start over again, and declaring bankruptcy can help.

What you are saying, however, is that declaring bankruptcy is not a decision that is to be taken lightly?
Declaring bankruptcy is one of the most important financial actions you can take in your whole life. For that reason, you must understand the magnitude of what you are doing, or about to do. You must understand what it is you are asking of other people. You must understand the sacrifice you are making, as well as what you will gain. There is a time and a place for declaring bankruptcy; otherwise, we would not have an allowance for it in our legal system. If you decide that bankruptcy is the right solution for you, I hope that you have explored all your options and concluded that it is your only way out, that you are aware of the implications of your decision—for yourself and others—and that you will start over from a place of pride and courage, not one of shame.

What is involuntary bankruptcy?
Involuntary bankruptcy is a situation in which your creditors, as opposed to you, file the petition for bankruptcy.

Bankruptcy sounds like an easy answer to all my problems! Is it?
If you think bankruptcy is an easy way out of your debts, think again. It is as far from the easy way out as anything I can think of—it brings a whole new set of complications and difficulties into your already complicated and difficult life.

First of all, try to imagine what declaring bankruptcy will do to your credit report. You will find it extremely difficult, if not impossible, to get credit from a variety of sources who once were begging to go into business with you. It will be difficult, if not impossible, for you to rent an apartment, buy a house, or write checks without a credit card—since you'll probably have great difficulty getting a credit card following a bankruptcy. It is extremely likely that you will lose property you had counted on keeping for a long time. And in many cases, someone else—perhaps a friend, a spouse, or a cosignee—will be saddled with your debts.

Is there a minimum amount of debt you can be in before filing?

No, there is not. An attorney I know sees people who file for Chapter 7 and Chapter 13 bankruptcy with debts of as little as $5,000, though I wouldn't recommend it, since your debts should be enough to justify the legal expenses you will incur in filing.

Should I contact a lawyer before I consider filing for bankruptcy?

Definitely. Before you do anything, check with an attorney who can explain the pros and cons of filing for bankruptcy and who can explain the differences between the kinds of bankruptcy that exist for today's consumer.

What are the main differences between various kinds of bankruptcy?

There are several kinds of personal bankruptcy. Chapter 7 and Chapter 13 bankruptcies are by far the most common. Chapter 12 bankruptcy applies to farmers, and Chapter 11 bankruptcy is often used by major corporations who have gone under.

What is Chapter 7 bankruptcy?

Chapter 7 bankruptcy is the most common type of bankruptcy. Under Chapter 7 bankruptcy, a court-appointed trustee assembles all your assets, sells them for cash, and then allocates and distributes the money to your creditors. You can hold on to any assets that are exempt under federal law, and/or the laws of the state you live in. Basically, Chapter 7 is a way for you to erase most of your debts—but not without giving up some of your property.

How do I go about filing for Chapter 7?

First you must fill out a number of forms and applications listing your income, the amounts and kinds of your debts, and what assets you possess—house, land, car—above and beyond those debts. You can purchase these forms from a legal publishing company or even from a good stationery store. You can also find them in books about bankruptcy published by Nolo Press. You must divulge complete financial information in a petition for Chapter 7 bankruptcy. If you forget a debt, or leave one out, it may not be erased. Even worse, if you fail to list all your assets you could later be liable for fraud.

After I finish filling out the forms and applications, what happens?

After you complete the paperwork, you file a petition for bankruptcy with the court (for a fee) and a court date will be set. Your creditors will be informed that you have filed for Chapter 7. You will then be appointed an impartial trustee, a person charged by the court to oversee your bankruptcy plan.

Once I have filed for bankruptcy, will creditors and collection agencies stop breathing down my neck?

In most cases, yes. The filing of your petition "automatically stays," or stops, your creditors from garnishing your wages, emptying out your checking or savings account, pursuing you, or attempting to sue you for nonpayment. But this should not be the main reason you file for bankruptcy! And in some cases, creditors can apply for "relief from stay" and resume their efforts to collect what you owe them.

What are the responsibilities of the court-appointed trustee?

The trustee is responsible for all your financial affairs after you have petitioned for Chapter 7. A month or so after you have filed, you will attend a short hearing attended by your creditors and your trustee. This hearing is a question-and-answer period in which the creditors are given a good look at what you own and at the extent of your debts. After the hearing, the trustee will arrange to sell off your nonexempt property. This could include some equity in your home and your car, a portion of your property, and a certain amount of cash. Your trustee will then divide the proceeds among your lenders and creditors.

Are all debts considered the same in bankruptcy court?

No. By law, debts are divided into two categories: dischargeable and non-dischargeable. A court will determine how the law applies to your debts. Dischargeable debts are those debts that you are not legally liable to make good on after the bankruptcy proceeding is over. Non-dischargeable debts are debts that must be paid after your assets have been liquidated. A non-dischargeable debt is treated as if no bankruptcy had been filed, so a creditor can seek payment by any legal means.

How much will filing for Chapter 7 bankruptcy cost me?

The fee for an individual filing for Chapter 7 will be about $160 to $175. For a couple filing jointly, the fee can range from $500 to $1,500. If you can't pay this amount all at once, you can pay it in installments. You should also hire a bankruptcy attorney. If you cannot afford the services of an attorney, look in your phone book under free, or discount, legal services. Legally, you can always represent yourself at your hearing, but it is never a good idea to act as your own lawyer.

What kinds of debts can I get rid of during a Chapter 7 bankruptcy hearing?

The most common kinds of debts that you can discharge in a Chapter 7 hearing include back rent you owe a landlord; outstanding utility bills, including gas, electric, and phone; some court judgments against you (child and/or spousal support, for example, cannot be discharged); credit card, charge card, T&E card, department store card, and gasoline card bills; loans from your friends or your family; any outstanding legal or medical bills; and most, if not all, unsecured loans ("unsecured" here means debts that have no collateral attached to them).

What debts am I still responsible for?

Debts are considered non-dischargeable if the court determines that you incurred them due to irresponsible behavior or that you incurred them long before you got into general financial trouble. Non-dischargeable debts can include taxes and government fines and penalties, alimony and child support, all student loans, and any secured debts, i.e., debts with collateral. Any debts arising out of trouble with the law are not forgiven, either. If you were sued for personal injury while you were driving drunk, or if you owe any debts because of fraud, larceny, embezzlement, assault, or libel, you will still be liable for these debts after the bankruptcy proceeding. If you bought expensive items or took out a huge cash advance right before filing for bankruptcy, these debts will also be considered non-dischargeable.

What nonexempt property will I lose if I file for Chapter 7?

What kinds of property you stand to lose depends on the laws of your state, but among other things, you could very well lose (if applicable) your second home, your second car, any stock or bond certificates, CDs, or money market funds, and any valuable collections (stamps, coins) or heirlooms, as well as part of your marital estate.

What exactly is exempt property?

The property that you get to keep after you file for a Chapter 7 bankruptcy is known as exempt property. There are state exemptions and federal exemptions, and you can choose which auspices you want to file under, depending on which offers you a higher allowance. Typically, you can keep your home (up to a certain dollar value; in California, for example, the state exemption for a homestead allowance is $100,000), your clothes, your furniture and appliances, your personal effects, your jewelry, your pensions and life insurance, and your income from Social Security, disability, unemployment, welfare, and/or alimony. If you bought your car with an auto loan, then it is a secured debt that cannot be discharged unless you give the car back.

I am desperate to hold on to a piece of property that the court has just judged nonexempt. Do I have any options?

My advice is to try to "buy" this property back from the court, or trade it for property that is exempt.

What is a reaffirmation agreement?

Depending on your financial and personal circumstances, you might want to keep possession of a part of your property you feel you cannot do without, such as a car. If you have not finished paying off your car, it can be a good idea to "reaffirm" the debt. This means that in spite of the bankruptcy proceedings, you agree to pay all or a portion of the money to the creditor in question. In return, the creditor promises that he will not repossess your car, or whatever else it is that you are anxious to hold on to. Before you take this step, however, I would strongly advise that you contact an attorney to make sure you know all your rights.

I don't have any real property or assets to hand over to the trustee. Can I still file for Chapter 7?

Yes. In fact, typically most Chapter 7 cases involve persons who have few if any assets to liquidate to satisfy their creditors' claims.

What is an insolvency period?

The insolvency period is the three-month period before you filed for bankruptcy. This is also known as a look-back period. A trustee, or a judge, will examine your payments during this period to see whether you showed preference to some creditors. For example, did you pay back your aunt Milly the $500 you owed her but claim poverty when Visa and American Express asked for what you owed them? If it is found you engaged in avoidable preference, the money will be returned to the court and distributed proportionally among your creditors.

My property has been liquidated and the proceeds distributed. Now what?

Now the court will arrange for a final hearing. At that point, it will usually discharge your remaining debts.

What does "discharge my debts" mean?

Discharging your debts is another way of saying your debts are over and done with—history. You no longer owe your creditors anything, and they are forbidden by law to try to collect any unpaid percentage of the original debt: You are legally off the hook. Usually, under Chapter 7 debt is discharged within six months, often within half that time. You'll probably be informed by mail of this discharge.

Can a discharge ever be revoked?

In certain circumstances, yes, but it's rare. A discharge can be revoked if for some reason the discharge was obtained fraudulently, of if the debtor failed to disclose any property in his financial disclosure.

Are there ever any grounds for denying a discharge?

Again, it's rare, but the court can deny a discharge if the consumer has not kept adequate financial records, of if he has perjured himself before the court, or if he has concealed, or destroyed, or failed to note any property that because of the bankruptcy petition is now in the court's jurisdiction.

A creditor of mine is trying to collect a debt that the court has discharged. What should I do?

In some cases, this is considered civil contempt. Discharge is considered permanent. File a motion with the court that handled your bankruptcy filing, reporting the creditor's action and requesting that your case be reopened to look into this matter.

Can I be fired for filing bankruptcy?
Legally, no.

Can I go to jail for filing bankruptcy?
No.

Can filing a Chapter 7 bankruptcy stop a bank from foreclosing on my house?
Only temporarily. The automatic stay granted by a court will not prevent foreclosure. But filing a Chapter 13 bankruptcy will postpone foreclosure indefinitely as long as you continue to make monthly payments on your mortgage. Check your state's laws to find out if your state exempts personal residences from liquidation during bankruptcy.

After many years of struggle, my husband is declaring bankruptcy. Should he file alone, or should we file together?
The answer to this question depends on a lot of factors, including whether or not you own your property together, and what type of property it is. If you file together, you will erase your debts, your husband's debts, and all your jointly held marital debts. If your husband files by himself, that will wipe out his debts as well as his share of your joint debts—but it leaves you, as his wife, liable for your share of the joint debts. In community-property states, husbands and wives own equally all property earned or received during the marriage. Thus, even if you don't file jointly with your husband during his bankruptcy, your share in the property is considered part of the bankruptcy estate.

What about property I owned alone, before my marriage?

That property is not affected by your husband's bankruptcy.

My husband and I were divorced a short time after he declared bankruptcy. Am I protected from his creditors, or can they come after me?

If you live in a community-property state and your husband incurred his debts during your marriage, you are still responsible after divorce for those debts—unless the marital settlement agreement states otherwise. Remember, though, there is a statute of limitations, so if his creditors do not sue you within the prescribed time—usually between four to seven years from the date the debt was incurred—they lose their right to do so. If you do not live in a community-property state, and your husband has filed for bankruptcy by himself, you are not liable for his debts.

Is my IRA protected during a Chapter 7 filing?

IRAs are considered exempt property. If you are currently employed and have a 401(k), it is exempt as well. Other retirement plans are sometimes exempt, sometimes not, depending on the particular circumstances of the person who is filing, as well as on the judge's decision as to what is "reasonably necessary" to avoid your being destitute upon retirement and therefore a burden to the state. However, if you are 26 years old with no children and you file for bankruptcy, the judge may decide that your retirement account can be liquidated to pay creditors on the basis of his belief that you are young enough to establish another retirement account.

What is Chapter 13 bankruptcy?

Chapter 13 bankruptcy is for people who are currently employed or are earning a regular income from a pension, an annuity, or some other source but who are unable to pay their debts. Chapter 13 is a repayment plan executed under the supervision of a court, and it involves an agreement on your part to pay back a portion of the money you owe, based on the amount of your income and the size of your debts.

Do I file for Chapter 13 in the same way I would file for Chapter 7?

Yes. You fill out the same papers, pay a filing fee—usually about $175—and get a court-appointed trustee. But in addition, you have to submit to the court a plan for the repayment of your debts. The court will either accept or reject this plan. In the case of unsecured debts (debts for which there is no collateral), you agree to pay back at the very minimum the amount that the creditor would have gotten if you'd filed under Chapter 7. In the case of secured debts, you agree to pay back at the minimum the amount of the claim which the creditor is willing to accept, or else you agree to surrender the collateral, whatever that may be.

Do I pay the money directly to the trustee?

Yes. As in Chapter 7, after you have filled out a form listing your assets and income and set up a confirmation hearing, your court-appointed trustee will begin making payments to all the various creditors according to the terms of the court-approved repayment schedule.

Do all my debts count here, or are there exceptions, as was the case with Chapter 7?

Certain debts are not affected by a Chapter 13 bankruptcy, including child support, alimony, and local, state, and federal taxes. You also continue to be responsible for any and all regular mortgage payments. If you miss a payment, the lender can have your home removed from under the bankruptcy and foreclose on it.

How long does Chapter 13 last?

It can take three, sometimes four, years before your debts are discharged. Please remember that you cannot by law refile a Chapter 7 bankruptcy if you received a discharge of your debts under Chapter 7 or Chapter 13 bankruptcy in a case that was begun in the past six years—six years from the date of filing, not the date of discharge. (You can file Chapter 13 anytime.) If you get into serious financial trouble again, if you rack up substantial new debt, or are unable to make your mortgage payments, and it's been only four years since the date your Chapter 7 bankruptcy was filed, you do not have the legal protection of bankruptcy!

Can anybody file for Chapter 13?

If your secured debt is less than $807,750 and your unsecured debt is less than $269,250 (whether you are single or married), you could be eligible to file for Chapter 13 (for the year 2000). Stockbrokers and commodity brokers are legally prohibited from filing Chapter 13.

What if I can't keep up with my Chapter 13 repayment plan? Does this mean I have to file for Chapter 7?

It is quite possible that you may find that you cannot honor your repayment schedule under Chapter 13. You might have lost your job, or fallen ill, or gotten a divorce. Whatever the reason, you should contact your court-appointed trustee immediately. Depending on your situation, the trustee may be able to get the court to cut you some slack, particularly if your inability to repay your debts is only temporary. If it looks like it could be long-term, the court has several options: It could alter your repayment schedule to deal with your new circumstances, it could discharge your remaining debts on the basis of hardship, or it could convert your Chapter 13 bankruptcy to a Chapter 7 bankruptcy.

Are there any disadvantages in turning a Chapter 13 to a Chapter 7?

There is one very serious disadvantage: You must turn over to the trustee all the nonexempt property you own as of the date of conversion to the Chapter 7 court petition.

Which is better, Chapter 7 or Chapter 13 bankruptcy?

I think you mean, "Which is less bad?" The answer to this question depends on your financial situation. Each form of bankruptcy, Chapter 7 and Chapter 13, has its pros and cons. If you have really serious financial problems, no doubt you will prefer a straight Chapter 7 proceeding, which is used by approximately 70 percent of all people who file for bankruptcy in this country.

What are the advantages of Chapter 7 bankruptcy?

From start to finish, from the date you file to the date your debts are discharged, Chapter 7 is faster to complete than Chapter 13. And it gives people a "fresh start" (though not without a lot of drawbacks, as I've mentioned). In a Chapter 7 bankruptcy, the amount of dischargeable, unsecured debt you can erase from your life is unlimited, provided all assets and debts were declared and there is no suspicion of fraud in your filing.

What are the disadvantages of Chapter 7?

The disadvantages of Chapter 7 bankruptcy are fairly obvious in some cases and less obvious in others. First of all, you have to give up your nonexempt property, hand it over to the court, and allow it to be sold. Even after you file under Chapter 7, some of your debts may survive (those deemed secured and non-dischargeable and those that a creditor feels were incurred with the intention to defraud the creditor), and you can still be approached by collection agencies. If a friend or a family member cosigned any of your loans, he or she will now be stuck with your debt—which is not nice at all. Once you have filed for Chapter 7, it is very difficult to reverse the process. And, of course, like any bankruptcy, a Chapter 7 bankruptcy will not look good on your credit history.

What are the advantages of Chapter 13 bankruptcy?
The main advantage of Chapter 13 is that you get to keep all your property, whether it is exempt or nonexempt. Your creditors can't garnish your wages or send collectors after you, and you are protected against foreclosure. In Chapter 13, you are allowed to separate your debts by class. Different classes of creditors are due different percentages of payment. You also have a lot longer to pay back your debts than you do under a Chapter 7 (remember, not all your debts may be dischargeable under Chapter 7). And if you arrange to pay back your debts in full, your creditors can't go after anyone who has cosigned a loan.

What are the disadvantages of filing Chapter 13?
Your debt, secured and unsecured, has to be under $1,077,000, as noted earlier (less than $807,750 of secured debt and $269,250 of unsecured debt). You pay back your debts out of your own income, which can tie up your cash for a long time. If debts survive after your bankruptcy is closed, you have to

keep on paying back those debts. You could find yourself in this situation for many years, which could have a serious effect on your future income.

How often can I file for bankruptcy?

I wouldn't make a habit out of it! Legally, however, you can file for Chapter 7 bankruptcy once every six years. Most Chapter 13 plans have three- to five-year payouts, so while technically you can file Chapter 13 as often as needed, it is unlikely you'll be filing more often than the term of your payment schedule.

What are the tax obligations of a person who files for bankruptcy?

What your tax obligations will be depends on whether you have filed under Chapter 7 or Chapter 13. If you file under Chapter 7, this petition creates a separate, taxable bankruptcy estate consisting of all assets that belonged to you before the filing date. Your trustee is responsible for preparing and filing any taxes attached to this estate. You, the individual debtor, are responsible for any taxes that are not connected to the estate (i.e., your income taxes). If you file under Chapter 13, this petition does not create a separate taxable estate, and you continue to pay taxes as you did before you filed for bankruptcy.

How will my bankruptcy affect my credit report? Am I wiping the slate clean?

"Wiping the slate clean" is a misleading phrase because your credit report will show that you filed for bankruptcy for seven to ten years after the fact. This puts all creditors and lenders on notice that you are a risky person to lend money to.

If I claim bankruptcy, does that mean I will not be able to get another credit card?

Years ago, that is exactly what it would have meant. Nowadays, however, the credit card companies look at bankruptcy differently. Some of these companies apparently seek out people who have claimed bankruptcy and offer them credit cards. "What's wrong with that?" you may ask. Remember, once you have claimed bankruptcy, you cannot do so again for six years. Within that time, if you get into trouble with your credit cards, there is no way you can get out of paying your debts.

I am a working farmer with a lot of debts to my name. You mentioned that there was another kind of bankruptcy just for farmers?

Yes. Chapter 12 bankruptcy provides debt relief to farmers who are strapped financially, as long as they have a regular annual income. Chapter 12 is a lot like Chapter 13. You file a plan and a repayment schedule, informing creditors of when you will repay your debts. You will continue to operate your farm. You can be eligible for Chapter 12 if you are an individual, or even if your farm is held in partnership or owned by a family corporation. But your filing has to meet certain criteria as of the date the petition is filed.

REESTABLISHING CREDIT

I got into trouble with debt and am trying to fix my bad credit rating. How do I start over again?

It's human nature to want to wipe the slate clean and start all over again. Unfortunately, this is not always possible. The most important thing is that you are facing up to your credit history—and that you clearly want to take steps toward improving the situation.

If you haven't done so already, start at the very beginning: Get a copy of your credit report and study it carefully. Make sure that all the information contained in it is accurate and up to date, and make sure that if you have closed out a credit card account, that this is reflected in your file. Double-check your Social Security number, as an incorrect Social Security number can be the cause of more computer-based confusion and misinformation than you can imagine.

Everything so far in my credit report seems okay. Now what do I do?

The second step is for you to do whatever you can to try to pay some portion, if not all, of your delinquent accounts. This sends your creditors a good, clear message. It says you are not dodging your debts, but you have a sincere desire to pay what you owe.

Can my creditors take me to court?

Yes. Many creditors are fully capable of mounting a lawsuit against you if you haven't paid up your account. Not only that, but they can legally take possession of collateral, and in some extreme cases, attach a lien to your income from work, or garnish your wages. And if your creditors take you to court, it will show up on your credit report as well, which adds insult to injury and makes your credit report look even worse than it is.

Next, contact your creditors and do some honest explaining. If you happen to possess any accounts that you were late in paying off, but that you are now able to pay in a timely, responsible manner, ask whether your old delinquency can be deleted from the record. Explain the reasons for your lateness in paying off what you owed. Was it because of a personal problem that has now passed? An illness that is now under control? If the credit manager agrees that your past bad habits were caused by some extraordinary circumstance that is not likely to happen again, you should contact the credit bureau and make this clear to them, as well.

Can I negotiate with credit card companies?

Yes. Do you have any accounts that are currently in trouble because your payments have been late or incomplete? If so, you are, strangely enough, in a pretty good bargaining position. Offer the credit company, or even the collection agency, full or partial payment in exchange for their removing any negative information about your account from your credit report. Some creditors and collection agencies may be willing to do this; others may not like this idea in the slightest, but you'll never know until you try. (In either case, be sure to pay what you promised to!)

How about trying to establish credit again? Is this impossible?

No, it's not impossible, but it may take some time. You might want to try a secured card. You might also want to buy a copy of one of the excellent books about credit rebuilding published by Nolo Press. Particularly worth your while are *Money Troubles* and *Rebuild Your Credit.*

Is it worth it writing to the credit bureau and explaining that what happened before won't happen again?

Yes, but keep your letter brief. Explain to the credit bureau the reason behind your delinquency, whether it was divorce, illness, unemployment, or any other personal trouble that is now behind you. This is also a very good time to get some new, positive references. The best way to rebuild your credit rating is to walk the walk: Pay at least the minimum (as we've discussed, you should try to pay more than the minimum) on your bank card every month, and make sure that that payment is in your creditors' hands well before its due date. Contact the Consumer Credit Counseling's Credit Recovery Program at (800) 388-CCCS for help in regaining your credit.

Do references from a bank help?

Yes. If I were starting to rebuild my credit after a period of not paying my bills on time, one of the first things I would do is open a checking or a savings account, or both. Creditors look at these accounts as solid evidence that you are able to handle money in a responsible way.

What else do creditors like to see as evidence that I'm able to handle money responsibly?

You need a record of stable employment and should have lived in your current house or apartment for at least six months. And even though I discussed the disadvantages of both of them earlier, I would apply for a gas card or a department store card, or both. Even though you don't want to end up making major charges on either one of these cards because of their high interest rates, gas and department store cards are often considered good stepping stones to establishing credit. And make sure you make timely payments every month! Remember, you are being given a second chance, and you don't want to slip up.

Can I try to take out a loan from a bank to reestablish my credit?

Sometimes this can be a very good idea, but make sure that the loan is a small one. Remember, you are trying to show your creditors that you are an honorable and consistent person who can pay your bills over a long period of time. Credit is not a right. It is a privilege.

What about applying for a new credit card?

If you have been having trouble getting a credit card because you have bad credit and have been afraid to declare bankruptcy because you feared you'd never get a card, think again. You may find it's easier to get a credit card following a bankruptcy. But if it was your credit cards that got you into trouble in the first place, you are really playing with fire if you apply for a credit card again after bankruptcy. You could find yourself repeating the same story and ending up in the same place.

My credit is bad, and as a result all the credit companies have turned me down. In the mail recently I got a solicitation from a company who offered me a "check guarantee" card for a small fee. Should I get it?

Again, there is no fast, easy way to restore a troubled credit card history, as you are learning the hard way. A check guarantee card is issued by a bank or lending company and guarantees to a merchant checks that you write, up to a specific amount. I would advise you to stay away from these cards, since you will likely only be covered for the amount of money you have in your account anyway, and there's no reason to pay a fee when you could simply pay with cash and avoid these additional charges. Better to look into a secured credit card, which I'll address shortly.

I've been turned down by credit card companies because of late payments reflected on my credit report. But most of these changes were related to an illness I had last year, and my HMO was supposed to pay them. The credit bureaus refuse to remove these charges. Help!

Unfortunately, this is a problem that's becoming commonplace. If I were you, I would write to the Federal Trade Commission to complain. If more and more people do this, maybe the FTC will look into the situation. But don't blame the credit bureau entirely—often it is hard to tell if a collection account springs from unpaid medical bills or from a delinquent health insurance payment.

After you write to the FTC, assemble all the information you can about your particular insurance benefits and submit this material to the collection agency. It might also be worthwhile to contact the doctor or the hospital in question and tell them that your credit is in jeopardy. And it is always worthwhile to provide documentation and an explanation—brief and concise—to your credit bureau. This will help to assure them that this is a one-time-only problem.

I have been told that since I have bad credit, I should try to find a secured credit card. Can you tell me what that is and where to find one?
A secured credit card is just what it sounds like: a credit card secured by a cash deposit, usually of $200 or more. The bank behind the card will generally extend a credit limit up to 120 percent of your initial deposit. If for some reason you fail to pay your credit card bill, the savings institution will simply take the money you owe them from your deposit. In the meantime, your security deposit earns interest, and, if you pay your bills in a timely fashion, you will begin to build a good credit history since the account will be reported to all the major credit bureaus. No one will know the account is secured—not even the credit bureaus.

Do you recommend secured credit cards?
Yes, I do. In fact, I recommend them even for people who are not in credit card trouble, since they are so safe. Of course, they are especially useful if you have dug yourself out of credit

card debt or are trying to reestablish good credit after a period of delinquency.

Are the fees and interest rates for secured credit cards the same as for credit cards that are not secured?

Consumers who have had trouble with their credit in the past may find that the price of obtaining a secured credit card is somewhat higher than it would be for other people. Generally, there is a one-time processing fee of $19 for a secured Visa or MasterCard. The annual percentage rate for purchases and cash advance is usually quite high, around 19.9 percent (fixed). You may also find annual fees for secured cards in the neighborhood of $39. Additional deposits will increase your credit limit with good performance, but your credit line will increase after 12 months even if you don't make additional deposits.

All in all, a secured credit card may be less convenient and a little more costly than other cards, because the amount of your credit line will be limited to how much you have on deposit, but these two factors may help to keep your spending—and debt— under control. If you've had trouble with credit card debt in the past, a secured credit card may be just what you need.

Following a period of bad credit, I have recently repaired my problems with credit card companies. Am I now going to run into trouble if I apply for a mortgage?

The answer is probably not. However, with mortgage lenders as with credit card companies, your case will be helped considerably if you can prove that your past troubled credit history was directly caused by circumstances that were either beyond your control or unlikely to happen again—illness, a messy divorce, a lost job. If you declared bankruptcy, your chances to get approved for a mortgage increase significantly if the bankruptcy was resolved at least two years earlier, and you've established good credit since then.

DEBTOR BEWARE

CREDIT REPAIR COMPANIES

In the classified section of my local newspaper, I always see lots of ads from companies that promise to repair a person's bad credit. Are these companies kidding, or can they really help people out?
These companies are known as credit repair clinics, and I don't approve of them. I think they prey on consumers when they are at their most vulnerable, and I also find their advertising misleading. There is no way that any company can entirely erase a bad credit rating, and the fees that they charge for supposedly performing this service can be exorbitant.

What do credit repair clinics do that is so bad?
One thing credit repair clinics do is appeal to your paranoid side. The world of finance, the world of big government, is not on your side, they claim, and with their enormous knowledge of various "loopholes," they can help get you out of debt. What they are usually paraphrasing is the portion of the Fair Credit Reporting Act that requires a credit bureau to reinvestigate any information in your file that is misleading, or incorrect, or incomplete. Credit repair clinics want you to ask for reinvestigation again and again.

What is the point of reinvestigating again and again?

The only point is to clog up the system so much that some of the requests can't possibly be honored by the credit bureaus and in the end, they will simply shrug their shoulders and give in. Is that a loophole? I don't think so. Not to mention that this approach seldom meets with success. Plus, credit bureaus are very suspicious of reinvestigation requests that look as though they were sent from a credit repair clinic.

What else do credit repair clinics do?

They advise you to dispute practically everything in your credit file. That includes your Social Security number, your address, and even your name! Some clinics will go so far as to suggest that their customers take on a new identity, and become entirely new people. This is certainly one way to get a clean slate, but one I hardly recommend. (In case you were wondering, under the new credit repair statutes, changing your identity is strictly against the law.)

Why aren't these clinics against the law?

Approximately 35 states have laws regulating credit repair services, and in some states they are illegal. If you are currently involved with one, I would advise you to walk away. There is no easy way to repair a bad credit history. What's more, this quick-fix method can prevent you from facing your troubled credit past head on, with courage and determination, and with the resolve never to let it happen again.

PAYDAY LOAN COMPANIES

I have very little money in the bank, though I hold a full-time job. Recently I got a bill from the hospital for nearly $600, which I can't pay right now. A friend told

me to go to a payday loan company. Do you know any-
thing about these companies?

I know enough to try to steer you away from them. Payday
loan companies have sprouted up all across the country, often
in towns and smaller cities, and these days, there are nearly
8,000 of them. As far as I am concerned, that is 8,000 too
many.

What exactly do payday loan companies do that is so
awful?

Payday loan companies take advantage of people who need
money immediately and don't have it, or who are between pay-
checks. Often these people have credit ratings and would not
qualify for a bank loan, or the amount they need is too low for
most banks to bother with. Usually people who come to payday loan companies just need something to tide them over—
$200 or $300. The payday loan company advances you money
on your paycheck—what the payday company calls a "short-
term deferred deposit loan." In return the payday company requires that you write them a check, which they will hold until
you get your paycheck. In exchange for bailing you out, the
company will charge you a fee of $15 to $30. Some consumer
advocates claim that this fee, if you calculated it annually, often runs as high as 780 percent of the money that you have
borrowed. A consumer needs only two things to qualify for a
payday loan—a regular paycheck and a bank checking account.

Are there any laws to protect consumers against pay-
day loan companies?

Unfortunately, many of these companies are not subject to
federal or state laws that govern lending practices, in large part
because they are such a new phenomenon. Many states outlaw

them, but they are still legal in some states. I would stay far, far away from these companies. They could get you into horrendous trouble before you know it.

Aside from the very high interest rate, what kind of trouble can payday loan companies get me into?

The kind of trouble that never ends. What often happens is that there is no change in a consumer's financial status when he or she receives his or her paycheck and these payday loan companies agree to extend the loan—for another $30. Sometimes people go to another payday loan company to take out a loan to pay back the original payday loan company. You can see how this could become a vicious circle of borrowing that could end up putting consumers in far more debt than they originally counted on—and with interest charges that soar into the stratosphere.

Debt is a sprawling, multi-layered topic that seems to grow bigger and more complicated, the deeper into it you go—not unlike the state of being in debt itself. It's a rare thing, in my experience, to find someone with "contained" debt—just a little bit that's manageable and under control. More often, especially in the case of credit card accounts, debt spirals away from us, growing ever larger until it threatens to define us. And that's when we enter truly dangerous territory, for we feel defined by it, ashamed of it, powerless to control it.

What I've attempted to do, in part, in these pages is to strip debt of its mystique. I also hope that this book has shown you that debt isn't always something to fear. There is such a thing as good debt when it comes to improving yourself and your life. No matter the size or the variety, debt is always, ultimately manageable. There are many, many resources for you to draw upon as you work to free yourself of debt: agencies to help you overcome your debt, break free of spending patterns, and regain control over your finances and your life; counselors and loved ones to support you emotionally; and information, in books and on line, to empower you with knowledge. There is much you can do before you reach the "last resort" of bankruptcy, but even if you find yourself in that unenviable position, it is possible—it is always possible—to begin again, to remake your life *your* way.

ADDITIONAL RESOURCES

CHARGE AND CREDIT CARDS

Here are the corporate addresses of the five largest charge and credit
card companies:

American Express
Office of the President
American Express Tower
World Financial Center
New York, NY 10285-3130

Diners Club
8725 West Sahara Avenue
The Lakes, NV 89117

Discover
Cardmember Services
2500 Lake Cook Road
Riverwoods, IL 60015

MasterCard International
Public Relations
888 Seventh Avenue
New York, NY 10106

Visa
Consumer Relations
P.O. Box 8999
San Francisco, CA 94128

REMOVING YOUR NAME FROM MAILING LISTS

Contact the Direct Marketing Association's Mail and Telephone Preference Services at the addresses below:

Mail Preference Service
P.O. Box 9008
Farmingdale, NY 11735

Telephone Preference Service
P.O. Box 9104
Farmingdale, NY 11735

COUNSELING SERVICES

American Collectors Association
www.collector.com
aca@collector.com

Consumer Credit Counseling Service (CCCS)
You can reach the CCCS at (800) 388-2227. Based on your area code, your phone call will automatically be plugged into the CCCS office nearest you.

Debt Counselors of America (DCA)
1680 East Gude Drive
Rockville, MD 20850
(800) 680-3328
A unique credit and financial counseling organization, DCA offers debt management programs, Certified Financial Planning®, and even a debt chat room. You can reach DCA at (800) 680-DEBT, or visit their website at *www.getoutofdebt.org.*

Debtors Anonymous
Debtors Anonymous General Services
P.O. Box 920888
Needham, MA 02492-0009
(781) 453-2743 (all calls are confidential)
www.debtorsanonymous.org

CREDIT BUREAUS

Here are the addresses, phone numbers, and websites of the big three credit bureaus, as well as the address of the Federal Trade Commission.

Equifax (formerly CBI/Equifax)
P.O. Box 740241
Atlanta, GA 30374-0241
(800) 685-1111
(800) 997-2493 for residents of Colorado, Georgia, Maryland, Massachusetts, New Jersey, or Vermont
www.equifax.com/consumer/consumer.html

Experian (formerly TRW Information Systems, Inc.)
P.O. Box 2104
Allen, TX 75013-2104
(800) EXPERIAN
www.experian.com

Trans Union Corporation
Consumer Disclosure Center
P.O. Box 403
Springfield, PA 19064-0390
(800) 888-4213 to get your credit report
(800) 916-8800 to ask questions about your report
www.tuc.com

Federal Trade Commission, Main Office
6th Street & Pennsylvania Avenue, NW
Washington, DC 20580
www.ftc.gov

LOANS

For information on Perkins, Stafford, and PLUS loans, contact:

U.S. Department of Education
400 Maryland Avenue, SW
Washington, DC 20202-0498
(800) USA-LEARN
www.ed.gov

To report harassment by debt collectors, contact the Deputy Director of Debt Collections at (202) 708-4766. If harassment continues, call the Policy Development Division of the Loan Branch of the Department of Education, (202) 708-8242.

ADDITIONAL READING

Chapter 13 Bankruptcy: Repay Your Debts, 4th edition (Berkeley, CA: Nolo Press, 1999), Robin Leonard
Attorney Leonard is back with a comprehensive and trustworthy guide to the ins and outs of filing for Chapter 13 bankruptcy. You can write or call Nolo Press at 930 Parker Street, Berkeley, CA 94710, (800) 992-6656, or access their website at *www.nolo.com.*

How to File for Chapter 7 Bankruptcy, 8th edition (Berkeley, CA: Nolo Press, 1999), Stephen Elias, Albin Renauer, and Robin Leonard
The best guide out there to filing for Chapter 7 bankruptcy.

Money Troubles: Legal Strategies to Cope with Your Debts, 5th edition (Berkeley, CA: Nolo Press, 1999), Robin Leonard
A comprehensive step-by-step guide to facing and dealing head-on with your debts.

The Ultimate Credit Handbook: How to Double Your Credit, Cut Your Debt, and Have a Lifetime of Great Credit, 2nd edition (New York: Plume, 1997), Gerri Detweiler
The definitive and most up-to-date resource for getting, keeping, and managing credit.

WEBSITE

www.debtfree.org
A great resource for consumers to learn how to correct their credit report.

INDEX

ABOUT THE AUTHOR

Suze Orman is the author of the #1 *New York Times* bestsellers *The 9 Steps to Financial Freedom* and *The Courage to Be Rich* and the national bestseller *You've Earned It, Don't Lose It.* A Certified Financial Planner®, she directed the Suze Orman Financial Group from 1987 to 1997, served as Vice President of Investments for Prudential Bache Securities from 1983 to 1987, and from 1980 to 1983 was an account executive at Merrill Lynch. She has hosted two PBS specials, one based on *The 9 Steps to Financial Freedom* and the other on *The Courage to Be Rich,* and is currently a financial contributor to NBC News' *Today.* She lectures widely throughout the United States and has appeared on *Dateline,* CNN, and CNBC, and has made numerous appearances on *The Oprah Winfrey Show.*